graft

motherhood,
family and
a year on the land

maggie
mackellar

Illustrations by Sarah Bird

PENGUIN BOOKS

PENGUIN BOOKS

UK | USA | Canada | Ireland | Australia
India | New Zealand | South Africa | China

Penguin Books is part of the Penguin Random House group of companies whose addresses can be found at global.penguinrandomhouse.com

First published by Hamish Hamilton in 2023
This edition published by Penguin Books, 2024

Cover photography, 'Ewe and Lambs in Barn',
by Kim Zumwalt, courtesy of Getty Images
Cover design by Adam Laszczuk © Penguin Random House Australia Pty Ltd
Internal design by Post Pre-press Group, Australia
Typeset in Adobe Garamond Pro by Post Pre-press Group, Australia

Printed and bound in Australia by Griffin Press, an accredited ISO AS/NZS 14001 Environmental Management Systems printer

A catalogue record for this book is available from the National Library of Australia

ISBN 978 1 76134 92 18

This project was assisted by the Copyright Agency Cultural Fund

penguin.com.au

We at Penguin Random House Australia acknowledge that Aboriginal and Torres Strait Islander peoples are the Traditional Custodians and the first storytellers of the lands on which we live and work. We honour Aboriginal and Torres Strait Islander peoples' continuous connection to Country, waters, skies and communities. We celebrate Aboriginal and Torres Strait Islander stories, traditions and living cultures; and we pay our respects to Elders past and present.

'In *Graft*, MacKellar asks us to pay attention to the world, in all its splendour and its darkness ... There is great beauty here. A book of uncommon sensitivity and attentiveness. Vital and compelling.' – Jessie Cole

'Maggie MacKellar's words are such a gift: tough, delicate, evocative meditative, poetic and resilient.' – Sophie Cunningham

'Two works of non-fiction made my hair stand on end: *Graft*, by Maggie MacKellar, a beautiful, poetic page turner about a year on a Tasmanian coastal sheep farm, rich and deep with observation and emotion.' – Geraldine Brooks, *Sydney Morning Herald*, Best Books of 2023

'*Graft* by Maggie MacKellar is an absolute standout, a beautiful account of a year on a farm, that weaves place, family and memoir.' – Anna Clark, *Sydney Morning Herald*, Best Books of 2023

'An often fierce, unflinching account of four seasons of a drought year on a sheep farm on Tasmania's East Coast. What beauty it finds – and there is much beauty here too ... passages locate *Graft* in the tradition of nature writing that emerges with Thoreau and continues in such contemporary writers of place as Annie Dillard and Barry Lopez. What makes it different is that such fine noticing is braided here with the pragmatic obligations of rural life ... And as the creeks run again and the pasture returns, so too does a renewed sense of hope and purpose for the author of this brave and bittersweet book.' – Geordie Williamson, *Australian*

'To attempt to sum up this beautiful book is to do a disservice to the delicate and finely woven lattice of narrative threads that comprise it, like reducing a glimmering spider web to its geometry ... MacKellar dwells close to the earth and it seeps out through her words, inspiring one to reflect on how each of us makes our peace with living between the domestic and the wild.' – Fiona Capp, *Sydney Morning Herald*

ALSO BY MAGGIE MACKELLAR

How to Get There
When It Rains
Strangers in a Foreign Land
Core of My Heart, My Country

This work was written from my home on the unceded country of the paredarerme nation of lutruwita/trouwunna. I pay my respects to the first storytellers, and all palawa Elders past and present.

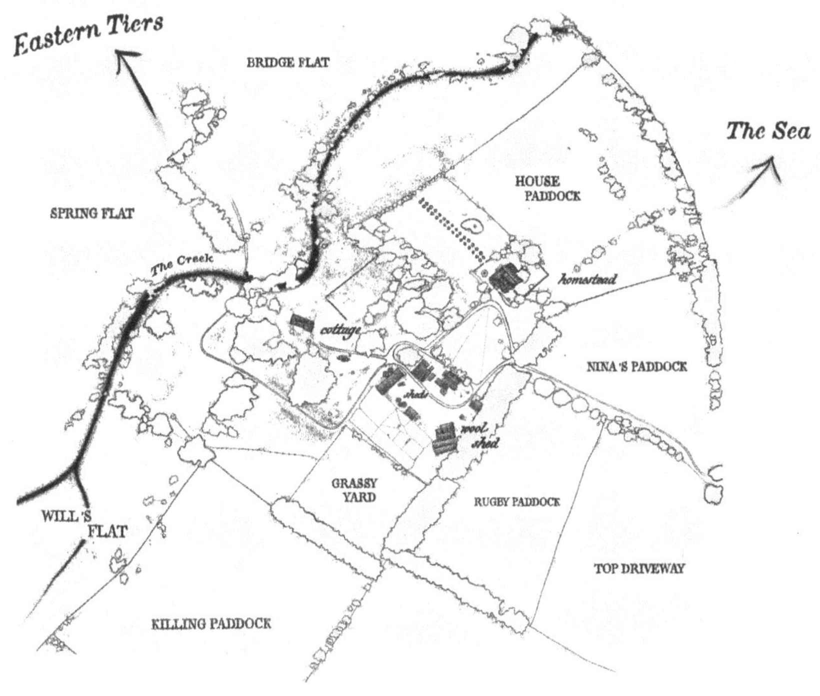

Map of The Homestead

and surrounding yards

Where you come from is gone, where you thought you were going never was there, and where you are is no good unless you can get away from it. Where is there a place for you to be?

No place. Nothing outside you can give you any place.

Flannery O'Connor, *Wise Blood*

Wiradjuri country,
Central West New South Wales

In my mind I walk over the land. I run my hands through the grass as if it were the hair on my head. I dig my fingers into the dirt as if the soil were the crust of my skin. My thoughts are traced by ants. Birds fly out my ears. Willie wagtail, morepork, magpie, rufous whistler, pied butcherbird, tinkling of crested pigeon. A yellowbox grows thick around my waist, messy with limbs and riotous green. My feet sprout roots which reach secret rivers beyond the creek bed, tasting hidden water fat with minerals. Soft thud of wallaby on my heart, pad of wombat. I am alive with sound and swollen with meaning.

THIS STORY STARTS TWENTY YEARS AGO with the birth of my son. When he was only hours old, my mother and my friend whispered their leave and left he and I to learn each other. In the quiet, the spectre of my husband's death, only ten weeks earlier, hovered over us. I lay in the bed and looked into the dark, and then I turned and looked at my perfect baby.

In every memory of this moment, I whisper words of encouragement. And my twenty-eight-year-old self reaches for that baby and believes my thirty-eight-year-old self, my forty-eight-year-old self, my sixty-year-old self – all of these women whispering back to that young woman. *Don't panic. Pick up the baby. Run your lips over his down. Let each perfect feature, the depth in his eyes, the quiet intensity of him, fill you. Tell him he's safe; tell him you are too.*

Later, my mother brought my daughter to meet her new brother, and my daughter's blue eyes, the imprint of her dead father, *their* dead father, only strengthened my resolve. This was now my calling. Ambition be damned. Career be damned. The only thing that lay in front of me was to mother these children. And oh how I failed. And yet, and yet, I succeeded.

Which brings me to now. To this moment when I prepare to watch my newly adult son drive away. As I do, I take my place in the long lineage of women who have waved their children off into the world. The sheer beauty of him washes over me, just as it did when we first met. We hug. He steps into the vehicle. This is big, he says. It is, I say.

He gathers himself, and in his almost-man arrogance, the careless grace of strength and vigour, he takes a deep breath, and in the next moment he's gone.

I stand alone, small and old.

The dogs are gathered round. Hovering at my edges, aware I am leaking. I take the laundry basket. Stand under the clothesline. Remove the sheets. Hear what might have been the whisper of my fifty-eight-year-old self, my sixty-eight-year-old self: *fold the washing, let the tears fall. Go inside. Open your notebook. Write it down. Run a bath. Lie in it. Listen to the crows. To the wind. Let him go.*

And me? I am hollowed by his going. By my children's passage through me and out into the world. With their birth I put on the cloak of motherhood and now it's time to take it off. I feel naked without it, a person I don't recognise. They'll be back, of course, but never like they were when they were young. My body is marked by their growth. My mind, attuned to their needs, is like a drug addict, desperate for their progress, the scent of them.

In *Erosion: Essays of Undoing*, the American writer and activist Terry Tempest Williams writes about owls, but really her essay is about death. Ostensibly she is telling us of the death of her dog, Rio, but alongside this sits her brother's death from suicide. The two, the dog and her brother, were suffering. One of them chose death; for the other death was chosen. To negotiate what this difference means Williams watches owls, and in watching learns. Once, when she was learning, crouched by the edge of the Great Salt Lake, a burrowing owl found her and gifted her a phrase. 'If I can learn to love death, I can begin to find refuge in change.' Williams calls it a cursed phrase. I agree.

WHEN I WAS FIVE YEARS OLD or thereabouts, my mother put me on a small plane and sent me to stay with my grandparents on the farm where she and her siblings were born and raised. I had always been going to this place. It was home in the way our red-brick house on the Northern Beaches of Sydney never was. Normally my mother would drive five hours over the mountains, into the western sun, while her husband worked his way into his ambitions. She would go home when she could no longer face the task of raising us, my brothers and me; she would go home when she could no longer *manage.*

To have been put on the plane alone meant there must have been some sort of escalation beyond the ordinary level of crisis we lived under. Perhaps my grandmother said, 'Send Maggie to me, it will be one less.' Now, more than forty years on, I sense in my dispatch west something else, an undercurrent of relief, guilt, shame, gratitude.

On the same flight out of Sydney was a labrador-cross Rhodesian ridgeback puppy. A gift from my uncle, who lived in Queensland, to my grandfather. The puppy was ink-black with a white star on his chest and would be the last in a long line of labradors my grandfather kept.

We arrived, the puppy and I, a little travel-crumpled and air sick. My grandmother was standing beside the hangars waving as we circled to land. She of the soft skin, scent of powder, aura of order. We drove past the cemetery, down the dirt road, across the cattle grid and up the track to the house on the hill. I put my things in the drawers prepared for me, each lined with pretty paper and containing a few twists of lavender sewn in a fine linen pocket. I felt special. Grown-up. My grandmother, Mannie, called me for tea at the kitchen table. Joe, the puppy, had a raw egg and some milk and I had a rock cake from the battered biscuit tin. Nothing was broken. No chairs were upset. No milk was spilt. I didn't miss my mother or my brothers. I never even thought of my father.

Elbows propped on the scrubbed pine of the table, my grandmother poured a cup of tea for each of us from the pot with its knitted cosy.

It was different being there on my own, without my mother or brothers. We usually stayed in the self-contained flat that jutted at right angles off the eastern end of the veranda. It had been designed by Mannie, and its big windows brought the paddocks and garden inside, in a way the house, with its deep veranda, couldn't do. From my bed in the little closed-in breezeway all I had to do was lift a corner of the curtain and I could see the garden. But now I was staying in the house, in my grandmother's sewing room. My bed was made up with flannelette sheets, a woollen blanket, and topped with a red silk quilt. Everything ironed crisp, just so. The house was small, but I didn't realise that then. With its pitched roof and that deep veranda, it felt washed with space. It sat in the middle of its world, looking north over rolling paddocks and hills stacked upon hills. To the south stretched emerald-green lucerne flats through which the creek snaked, its passing marked by the duller green of she-oak and eucalypt. All around the great expanse of sky.

This stay laid a deep foundation for a rhythm of life that made sense in a way the life we lived in the suburbs did not. I think of my small self, separated from my mother and brothers, but held between land and sky in this place.

A lot of things about our life in the suburbs did not make sense to five-year-old me. My father, himself a farmer's son, was rarely home. What he did was mysterious. On the occasions he was in the house he would work for hours at his desk, at tasks so important we were never to disturb him. Bottle-green bags stamped with the Australian coat of arms followed him from place to place. They were full of papers that required his signature. This work was so important that nothing must get between him and it. He loved it, more than he loved us, or so it seemed. He was a rare creature, my father, and in the way of things seldom seen, he was dazzling, so it was hard to take him in all at once. He would arrive and the familiar water of our family pond would slosh as we shuffled ourselves around to try to make some space. We danced for him, in some sort of attendance, our movement tinged with resentment. Yet even as we resented him there was also a deep desire to please. This push and pull creased me in ways I did not understand.

The 'us', my real family, the one familiar with the shared water of that pond, was my mother, my two brothers and me.

My brothers have eyes of blazing blue, thick brown hair and fair skin that burns and freckles. One of them is tall, the other threatened to be so. They love food and music. They love people and watching TV. They are extroverts eager to meet and be met.

My older brother has pebbles in his mouth instead of words. His tongue is thick. It sticks out when it shouldn't. At this time I am remembering, he smashed and grabbed and pinched and pulled and broke the world every day, over and again. His skin was too thin and everything moved through him so quickly it spun him ever faster until he fixed on just one thing and held it tight for hours. When we ignored him he used his shit to make his presence known. He would paint with it, smear it over the walls of his bedroom, walk it across the floor, let it sag in his pants, hot and stinking. He didn't care what people thought. He used the shit and the not-caring more eloquently than words. Because of him I learnt how to read a body. Because of him I understood shame. Because of him, for a long time I believed in miracles. Because of him I learnt that the shape of love is loss.

My younger brother has songs in his mouth as well as words. He too was hostage to the world of shit our mother cleaned up day after day. He, like me, knew the smell was there, under the soap. The smell of difference.

Our father's answer to the none-too-perfect conundrum of our family life was to touch down and take off again. He never really came home. When he appeared at the door it was to change. If he had a little bit of time between appointments he'd take off his jacket, perhaps loosen his tie and roll up his sleeves. Or he would shower and emerge again with his costume altered slightly by a set of cufflinks, a different tie, or a dinner suit. While waiting for our mother to feed, bathe and put us to bed he would watch the news standing up, or talk on the phone in his study. On the rare weekend he was home he would have a break from his important work, dress in his tennis whites and roar off in his small fast car that had room for only one passenger. It never occurred to me to question why it was important for my father to have a proper break from work and do something he loved when my mother didn't even have a favourite TV show.

Like an actor or a magician, my mother would change in the wrinkle of time she had between scenes. One moment jeans and a shirt stained with domestic grime and evidence of whatever my brother had destroyed that day, the next transformed, in a silk dress of richest green, or a long black skirt, her hair swept up, a slash of bright lipstick, her clip-on pearl earrings, a matching clutch, and she was out the door off into the night only to return smelling of stale rooms, powdered ladies and smoke. She would always come straight to check on us in our beds and tuck a single after-dinner chocolate under our pillow. The crinkle of black paper and the hint of sweet mint meant all was well.

I'm hunting for the memories of my mother and me when I was young. There are not that many and those I have feel like carefully polished origin stories rather than memories, like memories constructed from a photo rather than ones that were truly alive. Mostly she exists trailing in the wake of my brother, snatched at by his hands, pulled forward into him, swallowed by all the things he could not do.

So, what my grandparents gave me was even more precious.

My grandparents' routine, the way the day unfolded, couldn't have been more different from the chaos of our family life. Instead of waking to my brother's bangs and cries to be let out of his room, I would hear my grandfather pushing the tray-mobile, a little wheeled trolley, up the long hall. His progression – from kitchen to bedroom – was heralded by the 7 a.m. ABC news bulletin. I would lie buried beneath the covers, as, faint at first and then louder, he and the trolley approached my room and on up the hall until they reached my grandparents' bedroom. They would have their first cup of tea of the day, listen to the news and weather report and then, after the pot was empty, they would dress and my grandmother would pop her head around my bedroom door. Had I slept? Was I hungry?

We would have porridge for breakfast. There was a glass jar filled with stewed fruit, a bowl with bran in it and a jug of creamy milk. Nothing was knocked over.

After breakfast I would go with my grandfather. Out the back, where, beyond the garden gate, his dogs were tied up. He'd let them off their chains and they'd run like moths circling a light. He'd hunt them off and we'd walk back to the house and carefully reverse the ute out of the garage. The ute was increasingly dented as his eyesight failed, but I was too young to notice his slow pace, and it suited my curiosity. And so we inched into the day.

Of all my cousins, I think I had the best of my grandfather. He could be hard and gruff, and he aged fast after his second hip operation, but this was a time before then when he still moved with the help of only one stick. Perhaps it was my obsession with animals that softened him. We would spend the morning together and he'd tell me stories about horses he'd owned and dogs he'd trained and sheep he'd shown. I was just the right audience, too young to challenge him and old enough to stay interested in his meandering, moral-filled stories. What I didn't understand was that my grandfather was in the difficult process of letting go of his small empire and allowing his son-in-law and my aunt to take it over. The tension washed against me; I felt it, and discomfit, but my surroundings there were too absorbing and distracting. So if my grandfather was cranky, it was because of the hip or the weather, not a decision my uncle had made.

My grandfather's farm at that time was a Suffolk sheep stud. He raised stud rams to sell to lamb producers. Older now, his focus was on his show team, which he would take to the big sheep shows in Sydney, Melbourne and Adelaide. Together every morning we would feed the rams.

The ram shed was the old woolshed. There was a small board, which is what the floor where the sheep are shorn is called, and here the feed bins stood. My grandfather would scoop freshly cut lucerne chaff into the big steel mixing bin, then with a heavy shovel he would mix a bucket of golden oats. Finally, he would pour a thick molasses syrup melted in hot water boiled in the old kettle. Outside the shed, stamping, banging, jostling, were the stud rams. I would bend over that steel bin, my feet off the floor, my head buried in the sweet mix of lucerne, molasses and oats, and mix until my grandfather got sick of me and told me it was enough. I would line up the buckets, made from old kerosene tins with handles of wire, and he would fill them. Then together we would empty the feed into the wooden troughs. When the troughs were full I was sent to open the gate with a warning to mind that I wasn't trampled.

I can conjure that shed. It's as real today as it was forty years ago. The smell of sheep sweet and sour, the feel of smooth wood polished with the lanolin that hung on the edge of the sheep, the dust motes dancing in the early morning light, the powdered dirt, the swallows' mud nests and the rams.

After the initial rush to the troughs, the rams would settle and stop jostling for a better position. My grandfather would lean on his stick and watch. His stillness was a lesson. He was looking for lameness or a drop in condition, noting which animal was muscling up, which one had a presence and perfection of confirmation that might make him a champion. He'd take out his notebook, always in his top pocket, always with the stub of a pencil shoved into its spine; he'd wet the nib of lead with his tongue and write. I must have got bored, but I don't remember that. I do remember the peace of learning to see and not be seen.

*

I don't know how long I stayed with my grandparents. It was so removed from my other life, the one where my brother was spinning through the world, the one where the days were loud. I realise my visit has perhaps grown longer than the reality. But I also realise that the time gave me a touchstone, a safe place, a template of how I wanted to live. As a child I had no doubt where I would make my life – it was on my grandparents' farm, doing my grandfather's work.

That this didn't happen came as a shock only to me. Everyone else saw broader horizons, ambitions not yet discovered; they saw love and diversion. They, my parents, insisted I was destined for something beyond this place (after all, both of them had worked hard to leave farming behind) and that I would forget.

I did grow up and away. I lost sight of my simple child self and her clear vision. I married young. We lived adventurously. We hiked and climbed and paddled in Alaska, returned to Australia briefly to have our daughter and then went back to North America, where we adventured more. When we came back again to Australia my husband fell ill and died, leaving me to birth our son and raise our children alone. I faced my future as a single parent. I worked all the hours of the day and night. Dived into my career. I gathered research students. I wrote courses. I signed a book contract. I was climbing that ladder. Then my mother, herself blossoming into her role as grandmother and adored by my children, was diagnosed with cancer and nine weeks later she too was dead.

Though I wore the cloak of 'ambitious academic', actually I was drowning. I was barely making enough money. My daughter was afraid to go to sleep at night. My toddler son was so fierce he scared me. To have a moment alone I would lock myself in the bathroom, get under the shower and try to drown out the sounds of him beating his head against the door. The promise I had made in the moments after he was born to be first his mother seemed impossible to keep in the face of just how expensive it was to live on one income in Sydney.

Rudderless, I sought wisdom. I went to see a friend's mother, who was a psychotherapist. We sat in the dappled sunlight of this woman's inner-city courtyard and I told her I wanted to go back to the farm. My grandparents were both dead. My aunt and uncle were farming there. My friend's mother poured tea and asked me, why not? And I laid out all the reasons. No financial security. No career. Leaving my younger brother to cope with my older brother. Fear. The reasons stacked up. But I walked out of that courtyard with permission to go.

I took my children back to that country. And it held us while we healed.

Everyone who expected a different future for me is gone. My grandparents, my mother and father. So too the farm – sold recently. But not before I had the chance to lay the same foundation in my children. I took an exit ramp out of the city and gave my kids a world ordered by seasons, by wet and dry; I taught them that in beauty is redemption.

I left the farm before it was sold and chose to move to Tasmania with a new partner, a man who had another sort of farm, in a very different country. I moved because I wanted more. But when I arrived I thought this country might not be enough. That I would never feel myself known here. I have no familial connection. No handed-down knowledge. I'm a newcomer. What I've learnt, or rather what I'm learning, is that to be received in a place I must be alert, open. And I must be quiet.

paredarerme country,
East Coast, Tasmania

Even the name feels clumsy on my tongue and I stumble through it, my eyes cast down.

Prickly box, east coast blue gum, oak, mulberry, silver birch, grey fantail, scarlet robin, buxus, cherry, rose (many), yew, superb blue wren, eastern spinebill, yellow whistler, poplar, willow, thornbill, silver eye, wattle, apple, cherry, lemon, grey shrike-thrush, sea eagle, wedge-tailed eagle, blue spruce, cypress, boobook owl, swallows, pardalote, periwinkle, grapevine, catmint, scrub-tit, dusky robin, clematis, hawthorn, black swan, pied oystercatcher, masked lapwing, lilac, hydrangea, rhododendron, lilies, green parrot, eastern rosella, swift parrot, musk lorikeet, blackwood, gorse, grey butcher bird, magpie and on and on.

Here, I live on the edge of the world in a house of stone. Here, the sun rises over the sea and the sound of the surf carries over the hill. Here, the wind is a language sung by poplar and pine, by firs and macrocarpa, by oak and then, beyond the house and yards, by gums at last, scribbly, stringy bark and prickly box. Here, the soil is as light as sand and heavy as chocolate and we make war with gorse from Scotland, tussock from Africa, thistles from California. 'Here' is three thousand kilometres from the farm on the Wiradjuri country where as a small girl I learnt about sheep and was taught to watch birds; where the sky was the right height above my head and the horizon far enough away to take a deep breath.

Words that are useful to know

MAIDEN: a ewe who has not had a lamb.

WETHER: a castrated male sheep.

EWE: a female sheep.

RAM: a male sheep.

HOGGET: castrated male or female sheep with no ram-like characteristics and up to two permanent teeth (by which you should understand that they are young).

TWO-TOOTH: a sheep of either sex who has cut their first two teeth.

WOOL BLIND: when the wool grows too long and over the sheep's eyes, blocking their vision.

CAST: a sheep who, for whatever (mysterious or obvious) reason, is unable to get up.

SHORNIE: a freshly shorn sheep.

MICRON: a millionth of a metre, the measure by which wool fibre diameter (fineness) is described.

Today, we found a ewe cast. Her lamb had come with both legs back. She'd managed to push his head out but now he was stuck fast. J's hands are too big. I roll up my sleeve and lie on the ground. I slip my hand inside her. She strains and my wrist is squeezed against her hipbone. I'm pushing the lamb back, its life back into the dark of her. She fights me, her uterus contracting, and I hold the lamb in place until she stops. I push again until I have enough room to reach down and feel a hoof. I find one, then the other, and ease the tips of them up, working my way past the lamb's nose until it's lying in the right position to be born. I pull gently as she contracts and the body comes spilling from her.

Afterwards, I stand under the shower and scrub the smell of sheep from me. I can't escape it. My fingers are tender from pulling and pushing ewes, and the skin is cracked. I notice my breathing high in my chest, my lungs not ever quite filled, my jaw clenched. These are sheep, I tell myself.

Yet my body responds to the crisis of birth and death.

Each small emergency, the relentless progression of them, takes a toll. If I am weak, or too tired, or not observant enough, or careless, or incompetent, then they die. On the edge of sleep I keep hearing the words 'Get ready to run,' and as I take that dream-leap from the door of the moving vehicle to chase down a sheep, I wish I was a stronger, more able version of myself. Arms pumping, breath gasping, I fall asleep with the vice of the universe around my wrist and in my ears the echo of a bleating lamb.

autumn

Scarlet robin, *Petroica boodang*, 12–14 cm
Females: pink or red wash on the breast; large whitish
forehead-patch;
buff-white broken-arrow wingmark;
tail edged white.
Males: black above with large white forehead patch,
white edges to tail;
upper breast black, breast scarlet to orange-red,
underparts white.
In summer, forages in stringybark (or other eucalypt) woodland
(from stumps, low branches, darts to seize prey on ground).
In autumn/winter, moves locally to more open habitats.
Voice: pretty lilting, *wee-cheedalee-dalee,*
quiet tick, scolding chatter.
Nest: untidy cup of bark-strips, moss, grass, spider web, lichen
lined with hair, fur, feathers.
1–3 m (sometimes a skyscraper at 16 m), in forked, horizontal
branch;
loose bark, tree cavity, often charred.
Eggs: 3 pale green-blue, dull white, spotted brown, purplish
brown, blue-grey.

IT IS NOT SO SURPRISING, given our arrogance, that when Europeans first arrived in Australia at the end of the eighteenth century they assumed they understood all they saw. They pointed at small brown birds with red breasts who ate insects and called them robins. Their assumption was based on an unquestioned belief that all of creation descended from Europe. A mere two hundred years later, in 1990, two American scientists, Professor Charles Sibley and Jon Ahlquist, of the Peabody Museum of Natural History at Yale University, used DNA to untangle the mysteries of how birds are related to each other. The bird books, an increasingly bulging section of my library, use words like 'stunned' and 'astonished' to describe some ornithologists' reaction to the results of this study. Using DNA and DNA hybridisation techniques, Sibley and Ahlquist uncovered the fact that the world's 4500 songbird species, including the iconic northern hemisphere jays, mockingbirds, robins and thrushes, had ancestral links back to Australia, not, as our forebears assumed, the other way around. It turns out Australian robins are no more closely related to English robins than an emu is to an ostrich.

I live in robin country. The return of the robins from the high country means the start of autumn. We have four robins, a scarlet robin, a flame robin, a pink robin and the dusky robin, who is the only robin endemic to Tasmania. They are small, graceful birds who perch high and sally into the air, or hover low over grass in the pursuit of insects. They sing in wavering song flights, twirling ribbons of sound, daring the birds of prey. Their arrival from the highlands signals autumn's intent, and almost overnight the garden is ringing with challenges and the air is crammed with birds. I greet the first red-breasted arrivals with a reverent bow of delight.

The swallows, who've raised their babies in all the corners of this old house over summer, practise forming flocks and gather like strings of twittering fairy lights on the electricity wires. As the mornings grow crisp the swallows cease to be single birds and become something greater than themselves. I don't notice them leaving, just an emptiness after they have gone. Their going signals the end of summer, just as the arrival of the robins signals the beginning of the new season.

Autumn is our best weather of the year. It's as if winter, spring and summer have exhausted the appetite of the weather gods to blast us with wind, heat and cold, and need to have a little rest before the start of winter. Quinces ripen and I hurry to preserve tomatoes, pick mulberries, harvest walnuts, dead-head the roses and mulch the garden beds. It's also a race to make sure the stock are in good condition for the winter. For my old horses it's the time I start watching, as the weather cools, to make sure their summer fat doesn't disappear in the cruel pre-dawn hours.

On the farm, autumn jobs are crutching and classing ewes, which means sorting out which will be bred to a Merino ram (for their wool) and which to a Southdown ram (for their meat). We run both breeds, and they could not be more different. Our Merino rams have magnificent horns. They're hard, rippled like cooled lava and, like a thumb whorl, no two are the same. Beautiful, elaborate, deadly sculptures.

Autumn means it's time for the rams to go out with the ewes and the cycle of life to start again. Perhaps that's why I think of this time as the beginning of the year.

And this season, over and under all the jobs of the farm, the shortening days and dying leaves, the tension and focus is whether we will get a rain – what is called here an 'autumn break'.

Words that are useful to know

DRY: free from rain. Used when preceding weather has also been dry and dry weather is expected to continue. As in, 'It's fucking dry.'

DRY: not pregnant. As in, 'Those ewes look well.' 'They should, they're dry.' As in, 'Bet she's fucking dry' (while watching one ewe start a mob of three hundred running).

FINE: the absence of rain. In particular, fine does not mean *good* or *pleasant* weather. As in, 'Our autumn forecast is for dry and fine weather.'

A RAIN CAN BE AS DESTRUCTIVE AS IT IS WELCOME. A rain can be too hard. It can fall from the sky so fast the water doesn't sink in but slides off the ground in sheets. A rain in January (when it's too hot for the grass to grow), though still welcome, is not nearly as effective as a rain in autumn, when the summer seed has fallen and has time to germinate, or one in spring, when the ground is warming and the days lengthening. Autumn is the last chance for good rain before the soil grows too cold and the daylight too short.

Everyone on the east coast waits for the autumn break. It's the chat in the supermarket aisle, over the counter in the butcher and at tennis on Wednesday nights. 'We just need an autumn break.' 'We really need a rain now.' Talk circles around long-term forecasts. For all the talking and the hoping, I am starting to believe that there never will be an autumn break. In the nine years I've lived here, we've gone into the winter holding our breath.

This year is worse. It doesn't rain in May, or April, or March, or February, not a drop in January, we had a storm in December. The last decent rain was seven months ago. The ground cover is spare and winter is a threat. The length of the drought, the too-short run of even average seasons, puts us in the territory of climate change history – this is the new normal. This is our baseline. It's deeply unsettling. I walk with a knot of tension in my stomach and an ache in my clenched jaw. I hear J on the phone talking to other farmers. 'We're one day closer,' he says, talking about rain, and it makes me want to scream. How do we keep hoping when all around us is shrinking and dying?

Here, in the shadow of the Eastern Tiers, we have more in common with farmers working in similar dry conditions on the mainland than those in the rest of Tasmania. We are reliant on an easterly system for our weather. The rain that comes from the west and keeps the rest of Tasmania green brings us a cold wind and perhaps a shower. 'Westerly shit,' J calls it. Farming here, with our white sand beaches, crystalline waters, cinematic coastline, tourists, seafood, fine weather, is perhaps a form of madness. In this era of climate change the extremes are making it even harder.

We talk about not putting the rams out, but our numbers are low already and if we don't have lambs this year we will feel the repercussions well into the future.

Putting the rams out marks the beginning of the breeding season. For most of the year they run together, a mob of swinging balls and clashing horns, in the paddock near the house buffered by garden and fruit trees from the movement of sheep through the yards. I like having them so close. In the morning when I sit at my desk the sound of them pushing through elm suckers, nipping off the new shoots, keeping the garden in the garden is a welcome distraction from some work I have transcribing doctors' letters from my friend's gastroenterology practice in Sydney. The rams graze together in the early chill, and when the sun gets up they settle on the eastern bank, chew their cud and snooze.

On summer evenings when the light lingers, the thump of skull on skull echoes up the valley. One summer we lost two rams from fighting. They'd been grappling on the side of the little gully that runs the length of the paddock into the creek. They must have locked horns. Perhaps one lost his balance, maybe both, and they tumbled to the bottom of the hill. There, they might have managed to stand and work out how to get apart, but instead they rolled into a fence. Of course, this particular part of the fence line was the only dip that couldn't be seen from the house, or even by walking through the paddock.

A friend staying from the mainland found them. She'd been out exploring the creek when she came upon them. When she told me I knew straightaway it was bad, yet I questioned her: two rams locked together by their horns and both of them caught in a fence? Yes, she said.

One was dead. The other dying, his great head pressed hard against the dead ram. The struggle was all around them, in the dug-up earth, the shit behind the just-alive ram. They were joined in the way of one of those puzzles where you have to figure out how to unlink the entwined pieces from each other. I hate those puzzles.

Of course, the dead one was our best ram. Of course, the almost dead one was our second-best ram. To get them apart we had to reverse the tumble they had taken. The dead ram was almost stiff, the one still alive very weak. When he was finally free we took him home. He was distressed, his breath coming in sobs. We tended to him as best we could, but he died too.

I think, bloody horns. I think, what are the chances?

The Southdowns we use as terminal sires (from the Latin *terminalis*, from *terminus*, meaning 'end', meaning the resultant lambs are bred for the lamb market) over our second-class Merino ewes. These ewes might have some genetic characteristic we don't want to breed on. It could be that their wool is not fine enough, or there is a fault in their fleece, or their feet are bad, or they have an undershot jaw. At ewe-classing a pink disc is placed over their ear tag and they are drafted into the mob known as 'the fats'. Their lambs are raised as prime lambs.

Both the Merino and the Southdown arrived in Australia in the first years of settlement. The Merino was imported from Spain by the volatile John Macarthur, and the breed was developed by his astute wife, Elizabeth. In Tasmania it was another woman, Eliza Furlonge, who was influential in developing the Merino. Eliza left her home in Scotland to select 100 Saxon sheep from all over Saxony in modern-day Germany. She sent the flock to New South Wales with her son, William, in 1829. But when the ship docked in Hobart, Governor Arthur, realising how valuable this flock would be, convinced the eighteen-year-old William to stay in Tasmania rather than continuing to New South Wales. That the bloodlines of our Merinos go back to the vision of these two women pleases me.

It was the dour Reverend Marsden who chose the Southdown, a British breed renowned for its hardiness and dual purpose as both a meat sheep and for a fleece. The Southies are the corgis of the sheep world. They have short legs on a full-sized sheep body. Their ears swivel with curiosity and though their lambs are small when they are born, they grow fast into chunky little nuggets. It's a good cross for us and appeases the historian in me that coincidentally we're running the two oldest breeds in Australia.

Before the rams go out with the ewes, they come into the yards so they can be classed and drenched. J looks to see how the young rams have grown, what sort of style their wool is developing and whether there are any injuries. The oldest rams are drafted off and in a normal year they would go back to their paddock to enjoy ram retirement, for J is a softy and can't bear to put the old boys on a truck. But not this year. We have no feed. They will be sold.

J is nearly finished by the time I get over to the yards. The rams look good considering the season. J's been feeding them in preparation for their one job of the year, and the Southies particularly are defiant with the bravado of the small. They have no horns, so it is hard to pull up their heads to drench them. There is a brute strength to them, they are muscle, brawn and balls, and they're not happy being in the cramped space of the race. Eventually the job is done and we walk back to the house for lunch, leaving them to cool off. In the afternoon J will load them onto the back of the ute and deliver the rams to their carefully chosen ewes.

It's hot. Too hot for autumn. I wait for the end of the day to take the dogs for a walk. The country looks grey. If it were a person you would say it was stricken with some wasting disease. Everything is shrinking. Cracks appear in the ground, wind scours appear on the side of banks no longer covered in grass; the creek is dry, the holes that remain are stagnant and low. Skeletons shine.

On my walks I'm seeing more signs of Tasmanian devils. They were gone from here when I arrived. A contagious cancer had broken out in the population and this ancient marsupial was on the precipice of extinction. Many years on from that moment, and a huge effort by the scientific community and an army of volunteers seems to have saved the remnant population. A vaccine has been developed. Several cancer-free populations have been successfully bred on islands off the coast of Tassie, and perhaps it's nature too, for here they are creeping back. One day I walked past the carcass of an old broken-mouthed ewe. Two days later all that was left of her body was a pile of wool and an ear tag. This drought could be the reason the devil population gets a foothold here again. It's hard to hold this duality. Hard to accept that, in the same season, grazing animals will die of starvation and scavengers will grow fat and sleek.

Walking, I crane my neck and watch a huge sea eagle circle overhead as its shadow rushes over me. A mob of yellow-tailed black cockatoos flares. A magpie stalks through the dry forest of wattle and prickly box. A troop of noisy miners hops from tree to tree until I reach the edge of their territory. The sun is playing with the bare landscape, making beauty out of despair. The stalks of a miserable rapeseed crop have a golden glow but their shadows are dark on the bare dirt. It feels too desperate to be putting the rams out, too desperate to hope for the stirring of life when there may be no grass to raise a lamb.

I follow the sheep tracks through the hardened stalks and onto a grass pasture that was sown last year. It had a hard start, and then a rain fell and, despite the odds, the pasture established. Now there is still a good covering of dry grass and it's crisp under my feet. If we just had a rain it would spring to life, but at the moment, like most things, it's just holding on.

Ahead of me, bursting up the creek bank like a creature from another world, runs a stag. The dogs must have nosed him out and, sure enough, in pursuit come the corgis in a useless twirl of yips. The stag is still carrying his antlers and he gallops with his head flung high. We've got a lot of feral deer, and now their cover is shrinking and hunger is forcing them down onto the flats, I see them often. This stag is losing weight. He should be in prime condition but for a beat it looks as if the corgis are gaining. Then he reaches the edge of the paddock and sails over the fence, disappearing into thick bush.

I can see J in the distance. He has some rams in a crate on the back of the ute. He drives through the gate, opens the crate and the rams leap off. I watch them, their noses high in the air, catching the scent of the cycling ewes. They set off to make babies. But unless it rains next week we probably won't get a high percentage of ewes in lamb. Although the ewes are in good condition from being hand-fed, they don't cycle well when there is no feed in front of them.

I think their bodies are not so easily deceived.

I turn for home and a scarlet robin appears in the gorse by the creek. He keeps pace with me as I dawdle up the track. If I stop he stops; if I move he flits ahead, landing on a twig of gorse, a strand of wire, a lone dried thistle. His breast is impossibly red, fierce and brilliant as if he is drawing in the last light from the setting sun.

Have you seen a robin? In real life, I mean.

I remember being confused as a child when my grandfather pointed one out, a brilliant bird, so small and bright. The robin I knew was in the English story *The Secret Garden* – plump, ordinary, with a dull-red chest, a keeper of secrets. I didn't know them as the keepers of fire.

'Welcome back,' I say to the little bird, and push through the air, leaving in my wake the insects rising from the gorse, a ripple for him to follow.

There have been other times I've met with robins. Once, when I was out running on a track down to the sea, a small brown bird appeared. I stopped and bowed my greeting as we hadn't met before. He settled on a fence post, the better to study me, and called *choo-wee, choo-wee-er* over and over until I thought, ahh, plainest of robins, dozy, stump, Tasmanian or sleepy, olive-grey *Melanodryas vittata*, so nice to meet you.

Another time I was with a friend in the Valley of the Styx, where the oldest, tallest trees in Tasmania grow. We had our heads craned back, necks cricked and brains thick with the sight of high-rise towers of stringybarks. *Tick, tick*, like a twig snapping, and there shining in the gloom was the pinkest of pink robins. A sweetie of a bird. The blush cheerful, like a slash of bright lipstick on a plain face. A pink robin, I said aloud in the dark forest. And then he was gone. My friend, her head so full of trees she didn't see the bright sprite, laughed and thought me mad.

And then there is this: the female scarlet robin has been observed performing a butterfly flight. Its purpose is to attract a predator away from her nest. Imagine her, the dull flare of blush breast, flash of barred white, fluttering, a pretty, tasty morsel that draws the hungry eye from her eggs.

My mother's name was Robin – just like that, with an i, not a y.

A man's name.

One day, a long time after my mother died, in the time where I am prising my white-knuckle grip from my children's hearts – that is to say, now – a friend drops in on her way up the coast. She wants me to meet her new girlfriend. They are lit with love. I make a pot of tea and carry it to the table. Steam from the tea flowers in the cold air. My friend's girlfriend is happy she has been able to come up the coast, happy the work hours in her new job are flexible. I ask her what her work is. She says she works for a family who have two autistic children. Oh, I say, and my words trip, I bet you're a sanity-saver for that mother. She smiles and I think does not dispute the truth of this. I ask about the children and she tells me one of them is obsessed with throwing rocks. And so, she says, this is what we do. Together we throw rocks.

Oh, I say again, I understand, and I know she thinks I really don't.

We move on to other topics, and when they leave I turn back to the housework and the wet washing and it takes two days till the memory swims its way to the surface. I ring my younger brother and ask, do you remember when D threw a rock at Mum's face and broke her tooth?

He pauses. Yeah, he says. We were down by the creek having a barbecue, a cake … maybe someone's birthday?

I say, the deep hole just below the fig tree. The figs were ripe. It's my birthday when the figs are ripe.

He says, I remember it was hot and we were swimming in the creek.

D didn't like picnics or barbecues, the sprawling nature of them, the way time shifts and fattens as people potter, eat together, talk. His inability to understand the different way time can work would have made him agitated. Also, he would have felt left out because he wouldn't have wanted to walk across the uneven rocks to get into the brown water. He wouldn't have wanted to look for tadpoles or hunt for cicadas. All he would have wanted to know is what time lunch would be. What time would we light the candles, sing happy birthday, eat the cake. And what time could he go home.

The job of answering all these questions, not asked once but over and over, and not asked in words but in grunts and points and loud noises and face-smacking and maybe biting, because the answers won't be what he wanted to hear, all that would fall to my mother; as well, the job of distracting and entertaining him. My younger brother and I were aware. But, in the way of children, we were angry when he was ruining the day. Not that we'd show it – what would be the point?

I don't know how we came to be throwing rocks. Perhaps it started as a skimming contest and built to bigger rocks making bigger splashes, the game breaking down, as children's games do. I know it is the sort of thing that would have distracted D. He would have loved the heaving violence of it, the delayed smack of rock on water, the careless destruction. I imagine my mother relaxing for a moment, perhaps half-turned away in conversation with someone, distracted. He would have wanted her to share his absorption, his building excitement, his sudden joy at participating in an activity.

I didn't see. Just heard the cry of pain and my mother knocked to the creek bank holding her mouth with the blood dripping through her fingers. He'd turned and thrown a rock at her, hit her in the mouth, broken her front tooth.

It's not until I have children of my own and take them on paddock picnics, or to the beach or to a pool or a supermarket or a café – anywhere, really – that I realise how distorted our childhood was and how much our mother tried to protect us from that distortion. My mother never sat on the beach. She didn't have a sun tan, or read magazines, she didn't sit in an easy chair with a glass of wine and let the evening unspool, she never had a nap or drank enough at a dinner party to have a hangover the next day.

I can't stop thinking about the robin's butterfly flight. It is even more extraordinary because, as a rule, female scarlet robins are highly cryptic. When she is building her nest she will fly erratically hither and thither with a strand of spider web, a strip of bark, a tendril of lichen, waiting until she is sure no one is watching before approaching her nest. When she's sitting on her eggs she is so still, no longer a creature of warm blood and nerves and feathers. When her eggs hatch she remains secretive on approach to the nest. Say she has caught a juicy mosquito, whose tangle of legs and wisp of wings straggle from her wide beak. She'll first fly from tree to tree, not approaching the nest, but instead weaving a dizzying track back and forth until she pauses, waits to check that no currawong or butcher bird, no clever raven or watching snake will see where her babies are hidden. With all that care to move through the world unobserved and plain, that this little bird would flare and parade itself with all the pizzazz of a butterfly tells me something about mothering, about desperation and courage.

There is no sign of water as we drive across the stones of Dry Creek. When the gate is shut at the top (as it is now) it's awkward. If I'm on my own I always stop in the creek bed and get out and run up the bank, open the gate, run down and drive smoothly through. J never has time for such caution: he will stop with the ute almost resting on the gate, so when I get out I have to squeeze between the gate and bull bar to wrestle with the chain.

This time I can see three ewes on the edge of the timber. One has just given birth, the other two are fussing over very new lambs. We creep along the fence line and pop up over the dam wall and there in the pale spring sunshine is a tiny cream blob of a lamb. It startles awake, sees the ute and starts running towards our bulk. This lamb is maybe twelve hours old. It's had a drink and probably been planted on the sheltered dry dam wall by its mother, who had to walk to the feeder and then further to the one muddy hole in the creek with water. The lamb stops, confused by the sound of the revving engine. We watch it in the mirror as it turns in fear and runs into the fence, kicks for a moment and then lies still, caught. There's a group of ewes around the feeder in the distance. I wonder if one of them is this lamb's mother.

It's a tightrope checking the ewes. Are we doing more harm than good? Will we mismother more lambs this morning than we save ewes? We're so careful and we tell ourselves that if we lose a few lambs over the six weeks of checking ewes then it will be worth it for the ewes saved. At the same time, it is impossible not to be affected by what unfolds in front of us. The group of ewes who were around the feeders are now strung out walking back up the paddock, away from the lamb caught in the fence. Even though they are a long way off J kills the engine and into the silence spills the calls of perhaps twenty crows, cawing as they circle above us. The lamb has freed itself from the fence and is trotting beneath the circling birds. It stops, ears pricked, and calls. I can't hear it, but I can see the sound coming up and out of its little body. It calls, pauses, listens and then comes an answering baaaaa, *deep and urgent. A ewe turns back from the mob.*

They join up and the lamb, under the shadow of murderous wings, is safe.

Bird words

CRYPTIC

1. Having a meaning that is mysterious or obscure. Mystifying or having a secret meaning.
2. (*of colouration or markings*) Serving to camouflage an animal in its natural environment.

GISS

A birding term, general impression, size and shape, from the German *gestalt*, which means a complete shape or form.

Black swan, *Cygnus atratus*, 1200–1300 cm, span 1.6–2 m.
World's only mostly black swan.
Endemic.
Sexes similar, though the female is smaller
with paler beak and eyes.
Male has longer bill, straighter neck.
Bill: red with white bar near tip
(so bright it might be dipped in blood).
Seen in large flocks of thousands after the breeding season.
May fly long distances, usually at night in V formations,
with necks outstretched.
Pairs form
a permanent bond.
You will find them where there are swamps or shallow open water,
where they can reach
the bottom to feed.
I imagine them, underwater gardeners,
grazing the beds of lakes and dams, the shores of bays.
Voice: high-pitched musical bugle notes, often in flight or on water
sounding an alarm. Also, softer crooning notes, tinkling.
Breeding: February to September. Males bring nesting material to
the chosen site and
females build a nest like an upside-down cone.
It can be a metre high.
4–6 eggs.

I'm watching a pair of swans graze the seagrass of a bay on the north-east coast of Tasmania. The water is shallow for fifty metres from the shore and the swans gather in flotillas. They bend and dip their heads, plucking the bulbs growing in the sand. I squint through the binoculars, the definition so sharp I can see the water beads shimmer and slide from the crisp black feathers. Their beaks glow red in the late afternoon light. Their tail feathers curl coyly.

Where we live, at Little Swanport, there are no longer a great many swans. On our big dam there are only two pairs who return each year to sit and raise their cygnets. Then, one year, only three birds came back. The pair grazes together, the third swan shunned, until the female sits on the nest and I see the two males grazing close. All this will change once the babies hatch. But up here there are fifty or more pairs grazing the edges of the bay and then there are the young ones, not quite so black, easily startled. At night they call in tripping, tinkling notes across the flat, quiet water, their voices like piccolo flutes to the heavy bass notes of the timpani surf on the other side of the sand dunes.

EARLY ONE MORNING I LEAVE THE STILL-QUIET HOUSE and drive down to the beach. I step onto the sand, take off my woollen jumper, boots and socks and feel the chill of night under the soles of my feet. I've learnt not to think about the cold, just turn my face to the sliver of light on the horizon and start to run. We, the dogs and I, run in the silver dawn, and the beach unfurls in layers of grey. The horizon of islands and the jutting peninsula, so familiar in their sharp outlines, are wrapped in skirts of white. Forgotten are the heat and wind of summer; this dawn only hints at the brutish cold ahead.

The tide is high and the wet sand deep, and with each step I sink past my ankles, almost up to my knees. By the time I reach the end I'm hot and puffing hard. When I first arrived I did not know how to swim here. I was confused by the cold, by the dread of not so much getting in, but getting out. The idea of a wet bathing suit clinging to my goose-pricked skin was enough to keep me from even thinking about getting wet. It's three kilometres up the beach and I didn't want to carry a towel. I didn't want to squeeze into a wetsuit and back out. I just wanted immersion and was frustrated by the cold.

I figured it out. I watched the dogs, watched their complete abandonment to joy. Watched them racing along the sand and then plunging into the sea. They would shake the cold water off them and keep running.

It is rare to see anyone on this beach. The only audience to our presence is grazing sheep and a pair of pied oystercatchers. There's an old shooter's shack belonging to our next door neighbour whose paddocks run down to the sea. But the shack is set back behind the sand dunes and there is rarely anyone there. So I do what the dogs do. I strip off my clothes and dive. The relief is immediate. I'm out of my head and into my body. Nothing else matters but the grip of the water. It's so shocking, even though right now the water has not yet sunk to its winter chill.

I stroke out beyond my depth. I know it doesn't count as a swim. It's a dip. But lying on my back, the swell pushing up under me, I am alone. I can feel the pull of the water, the seduction of floating away. The release is waiting here. Virginia Woolf, her pockets weighted with stones, is not so difficult to understand. Then terror sifts through me. And it's not the kids. It's not J. It's not my brothers who pull me out. It's just the urgent beat of my heart.

When I open my eyes, above me a Pacific gull hangs. His golden beak is dipped in red, like a clown's nose, cherry bright but with a touch of the macabre. I backstroke, push into a small wave and ride it to the beach, letting the swell wash me back until the sand is firm beneath my feet and I'm delivered again.

It's always like this. The ocean humbles me. Forces me to seek forgiveness for my arrogance in carrying on as if my life were significant. I seek the bottom, give thanks and walk from the surf, smaller yet more sure. The dogs greet me and carry on as though I've been brought back from the other side. And perhaps I have.

Running back is never as joyous. The end of the beach is a magic space. I know it is not a secret, but I also know it waits just for me. Every so often there is a footprint. Other people walk to the end, they might sit on a rock and look out, they might swim, I don't know. I'm sure they come here to be changed. At least that's what this place does for me. I walk out of the water, stand in the air, put my clothes on and my skin wears its mineral blessing like armour.

The prints of my bare feet are intertwined with those of the oystercatchers, hooded plovers and the fairy terns. The oystercatchers flap lazily out of our way as we run back. Their earlier alarm at our presence is gone. We are accepted. We move through, not a threat.

I once had a friend who fancied himself as a fisherman and practised his art around the edge of his busy life. When I knew him, he dared to write. But what he loved most was to fish. It always seemed to me that he was a little different from the other fishermen, who were focused purely on the fish. Perhaps I'm remembering this wrong, but his favourite part of the whole exercise was catching the bait. Head bent, his bucket close to hand, he would potter along the sighing tide. He could see the trace of a worm in the sand where others saw not even a wrinkle. He would crouch and dig as the worm shrank down. I always thought that as he bent over those worms he was actually praying at an altar. When a worm nibbled, he stilled the piece of rotten fish he was using to draw it up, and when he felt it bite, he'd coax it, link by careful link, into the daylight. If he did it well, it would not feel itself move from one world to another. It seemed to me that he too was being shifted towards a different state.

Though the beach is empty of people, it's always busy. Besides the oystercatchers and gulls, the sand is bejewelled by the tiniest of scallops, their lips open to sip the moving tide. The tubby plovers escort us, flitting ahead and landing, their thin legs a blur as they entice us on and on until we are clear of some invisible line and they turn and skim over the waves and land behind us. I keep an eye out for the pair of sea eagles whose nest, a pyre of branches in the fork of a tall Tasmanian blue gum, is a few kilometres up the coast. Competition with feral cats, a reduced habitat, busier roads and farmers sick of losing lambs have combined to reduce eagle numbers throughout the state. The sea eagle is adapting better than the wedgetail. In the spring, when the lambs are born, our paddocks are like a picnic-table feast for eagles and ravens. It's rare to go a day without seeing the curl of claw, glint of white, or pantaloons of brown crouched over a dead lamb or hanging high in the wind currents, watching. There are three breeding pairs of wedgetails and a sea eagle pair on our boundaries. But today there are no eagles, only the heart-lift of an arrow formation of black swans flying up the coast. The white patches under their wings catch the sun and flash like Morse code delivered in wing beats. I stop, run forgotten, crane my neck and watch until they are a memory. This place was named for them, Little Swanport – there were so many two hundred years ago that they were the distinguishing landmark. Not anymore.

I was twenty-four years old, pregnant and back-packing through Europe the first time I saw a white swan. It was shocking – the elegant snake of its neck, its black-lipped eye and pure, impossible whiteness. I stood astonished. It's now a familiar feeling, this kind of astonishment. Helen Macdonald, the English nature writer, calls it a joy to see for the first time something you have known for a long time.

When my daughter was born – no, when I birthed my daughter – I felt this astonishment again. I knew my child would become separate from me, yet at her birth I was surprised she was not me; she was already herself. And I knew she would crawl, and walk and talk, but still with each milestone I remained stunned. Now, on the cusp of her twenty-first birthday, she has left me to make her own life, and I am as astonished by this as I was by her birth. I don't lack imagination, yet I am unprepared for how anchorless I feel.

The sand is deep. I stop the fight of running and walk instead. I'm thinking about the swans, thinking about what this autumn is asking of us all, about the adjustments that need to be made to survive this drought, thinking about who I thought myself to be and who I have become.

I know being a mother. I know the contours of the loss motherhood asks of you, the vulnerability tattooed like an outline of the child you have cleaved to. I know about fear and about fulfilment. I know about personal sacrifice and the wisps of joy in watching a child grow into independence. But though I have understood that I am working towards launching my children away from me, my imagination fails me again, for I cannot see what that looks like. I realise I will always 'be' a mother, that my happiness will be bound up in theirs, that as they grow older, my role has to change.

When I became pregnant I had nine months to adjust. I had the moment-by-moment reminder of my body's insistence that this new being was coming. I couldn't roll over in bed without being reminded of it – of my new role as mother. Then there was the pull of life from me, the fog of immediate newborn needs, as if the only thing I could focus on was a tiny gripping finger. There is little choice in this time. In the first urgent days there are few moments to grieve the old. But at the other end, two decades later, as the children grow and leave, a different adjustment is being asked of me. It's gentler, but equally disorientating.

The week before my daughter's twenty-first party, autumn moves in, as if to impress on us the seriousness of its intent. The silver birches, always the first to turn, are no longer yellow but gold in the gloaming. The poplars haven't coloured yet, but here and there, on the out-of-control grapevine, is a deeply purple leaf. On the other side of the garden the mulberry trees are ragged. They look exhausted after feeding the ecosystem of birds, insects, possums and us. The freezer is full of plump purple fruit. Even the renegade chooks who dare sneak into the garden are sick of mulberries, and the possums will now destroy what is left of the roses they had previously overlooked in favour of ripe fruit. The walnut tree on the banks of the creek is fruiting and every few days I check it to see how plump the bright-green nut cases are. They seem to swell and pulse with a fluorescent glow until they split and fall. Each walk I return to the house with a jumper full of nuts and soon it will be time to take a bucket and gather enough to feed us through the winter.

We have a week of sheep work. Not ideal in the lead-up to the twenty-first party, but also something I've grown used to. The ewes need to be drenched and crutched. For weeks we've been on fly watch and on my walks I scan each mob and report back the dispiriting news of newly struck ewes to J, who then appears on the four-wheeler to run down and treat the struck ewe. The flock is jetted (a treatment that prevents fly strike) after they are shorn in June, but as the days shorten and the wind doesn't blow, and the salt turns to mush in the wooden bowl on the kitchen bench, the flies grow desperate and lay their cruel eggs in any wet wool they can find. Maggots hatch and burrow to the skin, where they will eat the sheep from the outside in. It's a sad sheep that's struck, but like all herd animals they hide their weakness for as long as they can. My eye is in, though, and I'll see a ewe standing on the edge of the mob with her head down, twitching. Or maybe she will be grazing, only to snatch her head back to itch the flaming nerves. The treatment hasn't changed since I was a child and though the sight of maggots under wool always makes my stomach churn, there are very few things more satisfying than pouring the milky white oil over the infected sheep and watching the maggots curl and die.

Crutching is the sheep equivalent of having a short back and sides. The whirring clippers pass up the sheep's back legs, clear her body of any wool stained with urine or dags (sheep shit caught in wool). Then, in a fluid motion, the sheep is wigged, the clippers shearing the fringe of wool from around the eyes. The sheep is pushed down the chute and emerges from the shed with a clean bottom and her ears pricked in wonder at the bright world her wool has been blinkering her from.

Crutching for me means cooking for the shearers.

The routine has a pleasure to it. I get up early, but not to write. Instead I go into the kitchen and put on eggs to boil. I lay out white bread like a sacrament. Make ham and cheese sandwiches while the eggs boil and then plunge the eggs into cold water, just long enough so I can stand the heat nipping at my fingers as I peel them, but keeping them still hot enough to melt the thick knob of butter and spoonful of mayo, then salt and pepper and for an extra tang a thinly sliced spring onion from the garden. I make egg sandwiches, a chocolate cake (sometimes), get the lunch vegetables peeled, put a batch of party pies and sausage rolls in the oven and pack the smoko basket. Tea, coffee, sugar, milk, tomato sauce, mugs, teaspoons, something sweet, sandwiches, something hot, all lugged over to the shed to feed the workers.

I'm still surprised by how fast the hours from 6 to 9.25 am go. Morning smoko is 9.30. At this time of year it's often warmer outside than inside the house. All summer I've been glad of the house's deep bulk. It's always cool, apart from the attics, which alternate between freezing through winter and broiling through summer. The thick stone walls are the only insulation. So in the heart of the house, no matter how high the temperature outside, it's cool and dark. Autumn is the transition – it's still too soon for the fire (and the woodshed is empty), but the autumn sun, so delicious to sit in outside, is too weak to heat the thick stone. I rug up while in the house and then swap my beanie for a sun hat when I step outside.

This autumn crutching is also different because Duke, my kids' much-loved corgi, is not here. We brought him with us when we moved from the mainland and he quickly made himself king of his new land. He was not a straightforward dog. If we had visitors I would make sure to shut him up. He was happy to see new people, but some people didn't know he had personal boundaries that could not be overstepped. He would only just tolerate J patting him. He was loyal to me if the kids were at school, but as soon as they were home he came alive. He was their dog. He would lie at the bottom of A's stairs if she forgot to carry him up with her. He would lie outside the bathroom door if she had a shower. If C was kicking a football, Duke was there. He would haunt their every movement.

Other than the kids, Duke's other passion was shearing, and he got to know it was coming up – he would leave his post by my side and wait by the door in the early morning, and as soon as J opened it he'd be off to the shed like a sturdy golden bullet. In the shed he would strut the board like a prince and heel the sheep down the chute as soon as each shearer was finished. It was the one place he forgot all his inhibitions and anxieties. He owned that shed. He knew which shearers would tolerate him and which wouldn't. He'd come home for a sleep at lunchtime, and after that he wouldn't knock off until the machines were silent. He'd sit with the shearers while they had a beer, then come home exhausted and lie in front of the fire without moving. He'd be so stiff that he looked like an old man when he got up to go to bed. Without fail he'd be ready to do it all again at the crack of dawn.

This summer I ran Duke over. Killed him not quite dead.

Straightaway I knew he was too badly hurt to live. Is there any point in telling you the fluky sequence of events that saw him, most streetwise of dogs, under my wheel? I don't think so. I ran from the car, sank to the ground and keened. We wrapped him in a blanket, gave him some sedative we keep in the fridge to take the edge off the rams at shearing time, and hoped it buffered the pain for him. Then we drove the hundred and twenty kilometres to the vet in town.

Coming down Black Charlie's Hill J turned to me. 'It might not be as bad as we think,' he said.

His optimism surprises me in moments like that. I had none. I just felt the rawness of past traumas rise to the surface and all I could see was death. In the end we had the comfort of knowing Duke was mortally wounded. The vet X-rayed him and told us there was no hope. We said goodbye in the quiet white of the surgery and the vet slipped the needle into his vein. I was thankful his suffering was over. We carried him out to the car, still wrapped in his blanket, and laid him in the boot. We went to watch C play cricket. When the game was over C was meant to go back to the boarding house. Instead I asked him if he would like to come home to bury Duke and I would run him to school in the morning. He nodded.

We buried Duke on the hill looking over the house and shearing shed.

I'm still not used to his absence. He was a connection to the time before and he tied my daughter to here. How's Dukey, she would ask every time she rang from the mainland. I told her the news of his death over the phone. In the silence I thought I heard the sound of a root snipped.

With crutching in full swing, A arrives home from university and immediately goes to work in the shed. Her arrival means that the following day we will be hosting her party for a hundred people, for which, in my eagerness to keep costs down, I'm doing the catering.

By the next evening, the pig turns on the spit. I have a whole lamb, deboned and rolled and then stuffed with a mess of rosemary, oil, salt, anchovies and lemon, roasting in two ovens. The shed is cleaned out. Spotlights mounted on top of silos light the dance floor. Fire pots glow. I send mountains of food out of the kitchen across to the party. The bar is under siege. The kids laugh and dance and eat and drink. We make speeches. I feel overcome with emotion and plough on regardless. I drag my under-age son home at 2 a.m., send him to bed (which is a swag in the dining room, his room claimed by mainlanders) then sit by the fire drinking whisky with their father's best friend, who has flown in to be here for this special night. He has to be on a plane to Perth in a few hours. I'm so grateful he's somehow managed to come. We watch the flames and let the unsaid lie quietly between us.

When I finally get into bed I think of my daughter when she was five years old, and I was twenty-eight and pregnant with her brother. My husband, her father, was dead. She and I faced a new vision of our future. Now neither of those numbers makes sense to me. I think she felt the oldest five-year-old in the world and I her ancient, weary mother. Tonight, I see this girl outlined by young womanhood and this birthday is a milestone for me too, a moment to look back and see how far we've come.

Dawn brings a break in the weather and with daylight winter arrives. Wind and horizontal cold rain, which will freeze the stock but not be enough to fill our dams or creeks, and comes too late in the season for us to get any pasture growth. Inside, the house is fat with people and I know this is a day to treasure because tomorrow they will all be gone and we will be unable to hide from the reality of a dry, cold winter to come.

Last night I had a lamb in a pen by the fire who called so loudly its cries ricocheted around the courtyard. It was defiant. It refused to settle with the other lamb in the pen. This one wanted a mother. When I went to check the ewes and lambs in the yards, I took it with me. I caught a ewe who'd lost a lamb and put them in the race together, thinking I'd try to graft the two in the morning. The lamb was quiet – it went to work on its new mother, sucking away on her udder, its tail whirling. She was mild in her objections. I watched for a while. Most every part of my body ached. I left them. There was a niggle that I shouldn't.

This morning in the quiet dark I sat at my desk and wondered how I would get some copy written, a grant application in and all the lambing jobs done. I worked until the sky was streaked with a thin line of light.

At the yards I found the loud lamb frozen. It was in the in-between place, hovering above itself. It was tempting to look away, pretend I hadn't seen it. Another half an hour and it would be gone. I wanted time back and to have taken it inside last night. I wanted time forwards so it was already dead. I picked it up. It was stiff. The frost had entered it. I forced my finger into its mouth and the cold came up from within as if it were a tomb not a lamb. A spasm shook its small body.

The temperature outside was about four degrees. It felt colder in our stone laundry. I ran the hot tap and water streamed into the deep concrete tub. I rolled my sleeves above my elbows and lowered the lamb into the steaming water. The lamb hung, suspended between the worlds. We stayed like this for twenty minutes. As the water cooled I ran more hot. My arms turned red, the skin on my fingers began to ripple, my hamstrings cramped. I wished I had a big wood fuel stove. My aunt and grandmother used to put lambs in the warming drawer and the even, quiet heat of the oven would warm them perfectly. This lamb was ice thawing, and it shape shifted back into itself from frozen to limp. It was as wet as it was when it was born. I lifted it from the water, rubbed it dry and wrapped it in hot towels in front of the fire. It was so weak it couldn't lift its head and its mouth was still cold, but incredibly it feebly sucked when I gave it some colostrum. I put it on a thick sheepskin underneath the big wood firebox that heats the courtyard. I didn't know if it would live or die.

When we got back from the lambing run, it struggled from its nest of towels and bleated for me to fill its belly.

winter

WELCOME SWALLOW, *Hirundo neoxena,* 15 cm.
Other names: Australian or house swallow.
Our familiar house swallow: forehead/face/throat dull tan, upper
parts
glossy
blue-black; underparts mid grey.
Tail deeply forked,
with lace-like white spots on inner tail feathers.
Voice: busy chatter, tuneful twittering.
Flight swift,
slipping,
low and high.
Hawks insects over water.
Many perch together on an overhead wire, especially in autumn.
Southern populations migrate north
in winter.
Courting males
descend
on stiffly down-held, quivering wings.
Nest: open cup of mud-pellets bound with grass and lined with
feathers, fur and hair.
Often reused year after year with the same partner.

Just a swallow.
I catch one against the false sky of our glass courtyard roof.
The tremor of its heart runs across my palm like braille.
I walk to the door and it slides into air.
My empty hands are heavy.

A PAIR OF SWALLOWS – FAMILIAR, ORDINARY, COMMON – make their home in the woodshed at the end of the veranda outside our bedroom window. They are one of the seven pairs who build their nests around the house. Their shit is everywhere – on windowsills and sandstone flags; toppling towers of excrement evidence that it's a messy business raising a family.

Every year J mutters about knocking down nests, but he never does. I tell him we're doing our bit for the birds and I know he loves to sit and watch their aerial acrobatics as much as I do. I read that in Britain swallows, along with house martins, swifts, even starlings – all birds who build their nests in the shelter of houses, barns and sheds – are losing out to the many renovations all over the countryside of old buildings. Eaves have been blocked up, crumbling stone replaced, barns have been knocked down or converted. These are blows to bird populations already under pressure. I think of this old house as a shelter to different species and, though the swallows leave a mess, I make my peace with them.

Their departure marks the start of winter. For weeks they've gathered on fences and electricity wires. Thrumming into something greater than their tiny selves. Then one day they're gone. The world settles around the space they left and we carry on without a swooping swallow to greet me every time I walk out the back door.

This year, as if to emphasise its strangeness, the pair of swallows who raised their young in the woodshed arrive back three weeks after they'd left. Did they get to the mainland, find the drought even worse there and decide to return? I'll never know.

It's six weeks since we put the rams out with the ewes and the autumn rain didn't come. J is feeding sheep every second day. The rams are shadows of themselves, just horn, bone and pizzle. In a season as dreadful as this it's a gamble to even put them out. The ewes are holding their condition, but it's time to shear them. Their whole fleece is shorn, where at crutching it's just their face and bottoms. This will be harder on them than normal.

Every morning this week I've come to my desk in the dark, put a match to the paper and pine cones in the fireplace and opened my journal to scratch in words. I've watched the sky lighten out of my study window. It's slow, this time of year. The sky moves from dark to a strip of light, the colours erupt in fiery pinks and orange, then fade, and only then does the sun creep above the hill and through the bare branches of the poplar trees on the garden's boundary. There are a few leaves, yellow and lifeless, like tattered Tibetan prayer flags; they keep on, defying wind and short days. If we had a rain those leaves would fall, but there's no rain coming. I admire their tenacity and watch the sun spread faintly gold into my window and down onto my desk.

I have a week of cooking for ewe-shearing. There's a team of eight to feed. We're a small farm, but big enough to keep J and me on the hop. J spends days getting ready. Apart from putting the rams out and leaving them to get on with it, the last six weeks haven't entailed any sheep work. The drought has taken pasture improvement off the job list and J has been fixing fences, feeding and figuring out how to overcome water shortage problems. I check the ewes on my walks, look for the rams, do a quick count to make sure the right rams are in the right ewe mobs, hoping to find the boys with a gang of girls, or their noses in the air searching for ewes cycling. Walking, I see the ewes working hard for a feed, heads down, eating what I don't know.

It's not as mad as it seems to shear a ewe at the beginning of winter. Their fleece can weigh up to six kilos. Shearing them now, just as the rams come out, gives them a chance to grow a good protection against the cold, but not be in full wool when they lamb. A ewe in lamb, with a full fleece, struggles. She gets cast more easily and she is less likely to take her lamb to the more protected pockets in the paddock if she is ensconced in a fleece. Still, it's a worrying time straight after shearing. But our ewes have good shelter and they will get extra pellets and hay to fill their bellies. If the weather turns bad then we bring them all back in. J pulls every piece of machinery out of the sheds, and the sheltered home paddocks come into their own with their big stands of trees. The house becomes marooned in a sea of sheep.

Always, drought or no drought, the build-up to shearing is a little tense. And this year, to add to the tension, we are a good dog down. J's oldest sheep dog has to sit out this shearing. Boz has a rich mix of most herding breeds in his veins. He's the end of his line, the last of a breed that J has had since he was a seventeen-year-old jackaroo. Boz looks nothing like a classic sheepdog. He's heavy in the chest, is coloured like a beagle and he's not built for speed. But he's loyal and smart and was handy in both paddocks and yards. Most importantly, he was not easily insulted, which is a vital characteristic for any of J's dogs. But now he's deaf, can't jump and is more likely to get knocked over and hurt than be of any use. He must be locked in the retirement yard to keep him out of the way and he is not happy. I give him a rub on his head on my way backwards and forwards from house to shed.

For me, shearing is a time of confinement. Being a shearers' cook is a job I've never wanted and have embraced only out of necessity. It is not how I imagined I would be contributing to the farm. I've grown not to mind anymore. Our shearers are a pleasure to cook for and good food makes a hard job a bit easier. And shearing is a hard job. You can make decent money, but it takes practice to get fast. J says when his shearers retire he's retiring too.

The shearers arrive at 7 a.m. J is out the door before they get there. He will have the pens filled with sheep the night before.

We both obsessively check weather apps. About the only thing the drought is good for is that shearing happens on time and with no delays. You can't shear wet sheep.

The machines start at 7.30 and if I stand at the back door I can hear their whirr from the house. I get smoko ready, the same routine as crutching, and there's something comforting in not having to think, just get it done. I carry the basket over to the shed and it's a whirling dance of movement and sound. Music blares, dogs bark and there's the scuffle of hard hooves on the wooden boards as the sheep shy when a shearer pushes through the gates of the catching pen and grabs the next sheep. The shearer will flip her over and drag her across the board. In one movement that looks silkenly easy (but is not) he positions the sheep so she does not struggle, then picks up the handpiece and pulls the cord of the machine. It's a hard-won skill to position the sheep so she relaxes. Some of them will startle or fight, but mostly the process is drama-free and the wool flows off them in a curve of white. To end, the sheep is pushed through the shearer's legs and down the chute, where she emerges into the daylight white and light. The shearer goes straight back into the catching pen and grabs another sheep. I say he, but increasingly we have women working for us on the board as rouseabouts, as classers and I hope in the next few years as shearers.

Rouseabout is a word I love, but when I look it up I see the definition is simply an unskilled worker. This seems a ludicrous description of the job a really good rouseabout does. A rousie keeps the shed humming, the shearers happy and the boss relaxed. Like a hen tucking chicks under her, they gather the freshly shorn fleece and carry it to the table. They throw it high so it lands just as if the sheep had stepped out from underneath it. With the presser they skirt the fleece (take the belly, all the dirty edges off – these go in separate bales to be used for anything from socks to bulky jumpers, to blankets, carpets and furnishings) and then the classer judges what grade it is and places it in the right bin. The rousie is off as soon as the fleece is skirted, sweeping the shearer's board and picking up the next fleece. Each bit of wool, from the dirtiest pieces through to the purest fleece wool, has a place. The classer's job is to sort the fleeces into categories – AAAA, AAA, AA, etc. – and when there are enough fleeces in each category the presser will load them into the pressing machine, from which they emerge as a bale of wool. To finish, the bale is labelled with the property name and the grade of wool it contains. Each weighs around 190 kilograms.

Tasmania is renowned for its fine Merino wool. The wool coming off our sheep is destined to be used in high quality clothing around the world. It's prized for its fine micron, its bright white colour, its cleanliness and softness against the skin. Designers with a focus on sustainable luxury and Italian spinning mills chase Tasmanian wool. And it's here, in the thrumming, noisy shed that we see the results of careful management and all our decisions about breeding. When a fleece is thrown on the table, it still carries the character given it by the sheep who has grown it.

Outside, J is bringing in woolly sheep from their paddocks and taking shorn sheep back. He's counting, drenching and pushing sheep into the shed. His dogs haunt his heels. I feel superfluous, a non-essential member of staff, but this is silly because I know every single one of the people in the shed is hanging out for the clock to tick over to 9.30 and the arrival of the smoko basket.

My shearing menu is not extensive. The shearers love roasts; I hate them. I think it's because the roast is a performance, or the serving of it is. It's easy, says J, who turns up to carve, eat and get straight back out the door. I don't mind getting a roast ready. I enjoy the act of stuffing garlic and rosemary into the meat. I thank it for its adaptability, pop it into a hot oven for twenty minutes and then turn it down and forget about it. I don't even mind peeling potatoes and pumpkin. It's the flurry at the end I hate. Timing crispy potatoes, a gravy from the meat juice, and then hoping J makes it back in time to carve. When he does, it's a work of art; if I carve, it's not.

And then it's done, the plates come into the kitchen and some of the shearers settle back down around the table for a bowl of ice cream and stewed fruit, while others thank me for the meal and return to the shed to catch a quick shut-eye in a pile of wool.

When they're all gone I take my time cleaning up. The rest of the day will be filled with all the things I've put off while I've been busy in the kitchen. If I'm lucky I'll squeeze in a walk. The week always spins by fast and perhaps the best thing about shearing is I don't have to cook dinner. I have a sandwich from the smoko basket and J has leftovers. We're both in bed early.

On the last day J always puts on a barbecue and a few beers at cut-out. Once all the tallies are counted, the board swept clean, the last mob back in their paddock, I send over a tray of chops, some snags, a loaf of bread, a few packets of chips along with a case of beer. J lights a fire and stories are told late into the night. I drop in early on my way back from feeding the horses but am happy to leave them to it.

When I get to the house I rearrange the courtyard furniture into its winter configuration. I move the table and pull the couch around in front of the fire. I pour a glass of wine and curl up to read uninterrupted. Everything is where it should be. The weather forecast has no nasty cold fronts in it, though no rain either, but for now I'm grateful. J will arrive back at the house relieved, tired and more than a little worse for wear. The ewes will quickly grow a protective layer of wool and we are done with shearing until summer arrives and it will be time to do the wethers.

Words that are useful to know

WEATHER: NOUN

The condition of the atmosphere at a given place and time with respect to heat, cold, sunshine, rain, cloud, wind.

WEATHER: VERB

To withstand and come safely through. To survive.

WETHER: NOUN

A wether is a castrated male sheep, who gives us the most beautifully consistent fleece. Our wether mob are run on our marginal country, where they have a view and a lot of room. They are left undisturbed most of the year. They come into the yards when they need a drench, when they need to be crutched and, as summer breaks, to be shorn. There is a lack of drama around a wether. They do not demand the stage like a ram. They do not have to give birth to a lamb. Their fleeces are a testament to their quiet, even lives. Of course, they are the first to be sold in a drought. First to have their throats cut. But in exchange, when the seasons are good they are the most stable of creatures. No hormones. No responsibility. Just eat, chew your cud, sleep and grow a beautiful fleece.

J AND I NEED A BREAK FROM THE FARM. I can feel it in the brittleness between us. The days are so short, and lurch between heavy frosts and bursts of blue sky and weak sun, but mostly they are just different hues of grey. Perhaps if the grey skies meant rain we might not be so heartsick. But they don't. At best there's the occasional sharp patter of a few drops. I know we need to find a blast of light, of warmth, of a big sky and a longer horizon elsewhere, but it's always hard to get away. And if we go, we have to go now, in this tiny window when the ewes have enough fleece on them to be safe from all but the worst weather, and before they are too heavily in lamb. It doesn't feel like it, but spring and the intensity of lambing are only six weeks away. So we invest in a couple more lick feeders and spend a day dropping them out to the different paddocks. Another day filling them up and making sure the ewes have found them, and then we follow the swallows.

We will visit our daughters. J has a daughter living in the drought-ravaged town of Coonamble in north-west New South Wales, and another on the seemingly drought-proof slopes of the Great Dividing Range outside Holbrook. A is studying veterinary science in Wagga Wagga. C is still at boarding school. A neighbour will feed the dogs. We lock the house up and go. In the dark before dawn we drive the hundred kilometres to the airport.

Flying out of Hobart and into Sydney is always a culture shock, but there's also a comforting familiarity as I recognise the sprawling suburbs and beaches unfurling below us. This fades as soon as we are in the fast-moving crowd spilling out of the airport. I quicken my pace, instantly drawn into the commuter rush. J strolls, oblivious to the frustration he's causing. He's like a rock on a river bed and the crowds stream past him on either side. I take a deep breath and slow down too.

We hire a car and the sensation of being out of place grows. The sheer volume of traffic, the aggression, all push back my sense of belonging. We drive north over the Harbour Bridge and up through the leafy suburbs that used to be so familiar but are now so shiny I don't recognise many of the buildings. We drive past my old school and though I spent eight formative years there I can't see myself anymore in the slick signage, the immaculate gardens and state-of-the-art new buildings. I wonder if it's still the same underneath.

We leave the wealth behind and join the motorway. Sydney is stretching and the cars race with big city urgency. My memory of driving this road is that after reaching the Hawkesbury River there was a collective sigh of relief and everyone – the traffic, the speed at which people talked and walked or served you in a café – slowed down. But now it seems the boundary has shifted, for the waves of cars keep coming. We pass the Gosford turn-off and it's not until we get to Merriwa at the western end of the Hunter that I feel the pace slow. We pull up to buy supplies for J's daughter and stretch our legs. We pick up beer and chips, along with a chook to cook for dinner tomorrow. We have about four hours to go and the day is closing in. But something in me is unfurling. We climb up the valley towards the Warrumbungles and I can feel the waiting flat land on the other side. It's good and dark by the time we're on Baradine Road.

The car wheels crunch the gravel as we turn through the gate to the cottage on the banks of the dry creek where J's daughter lives. I put my feet on the dirt and a willie wagtail greets me instantly so I turn and bow – how can I not? – as he twitches his tail in the moonlight. As always when I get out here, I want to lie down on the earth. It's the smell, the sensation of a bigger sky above me, the horizon further from where I stand. It all nips at me – where have you been, where have you been? All the fears we had about leaving the farm are gone; besides, we are too far away to do anything. I fall asleep to the sound of the willie singing me into home.

We spend a day in Coonamble then travel together to visit one of my oldest friends, who lives on a station on the banks of the Barwon River. We drive through Walgett, where they have not had a drop of rain, stop briefly in Brewarrina to visit the ancient fish traps, and then on to their front gate. I haven't been out here for ten years. The kids were small, C had only just started school. My friend and I have a lot of shared history. Our grandmothers were great friends. Her aunt and my mother were close. Her mother has been a grandmother figure to my kids. We also share a love of all things furred and feathered (though she has an affinity with snakes I do not share). She's lived out here for more than twenty years and we don't see each other often, but our friendship is like a plait, our lives crossing again and again.

Their house sits on flood stumps above a billabong that has been dry for years. But a week ago they were lucky to be underneath a storm system and there has been rain in the catchment further north. News has spread that the river was coming down. Only this morning they raced out to watch the water push past the house. It mixed with the stagnant green puddle thick with pelican shit that they had been showering from for months. Despite the thrill of the water flowing over the river bed, the river still looks sick. The politics of water are complicated, but there can be no doubting that something is very wrong with the management of our river systems.

We set off for a farm tour. This is the first week my friend's husband has not fed sheep in fourteen months. After the storm the country is transformed – we can feel it alive under our feet. Yet as we fuel up, we see a dead kangaroo near the bowser. Apparently they've been dying for weeks, dropping from starvation, and the rain came too late for this one.

The four of us head out and drive along the Bogan River. A flock of Major Mitchell cockatoos rises in a cloud of white and pink. My friend says she normally only sees a pair, or a couple of pairs if she's lucky. Today there must be fifty birds. They are like a sunrise as they screech and bank away from the vehicle. Hours later, after we have inspected goat traps and shearing sheds and claypans and dug-out dams, we circle back to the house, grab an esky, throw in some beers and head out to the 'mountain' to watch the sunset over green floodplains that haven't been green or flooded for years. It's stunningly beautiful and my head is wiped clean of the stressful grey days we have left behind in Tasmania.

That night we sit around a fire on the bank of the billabong. My friend's husband cooks his infamous Mulligan stew; it bubbles away in the camp oven, licked by flames. We eat under a sky packed with stars. It's easy to imagine other worlds up there. It looks so busy, and so close. Beyond the light of the fire I hear emus drumming. I feel a prick of discomfort, as if I shouldn't be here.

American nature writer the late Barry Lopez wrote that walking over the Australian desert was like the beginning of a conversation. His goal was intimacy and he talked about engaging his senses – the tactile, olfactory, visual and sonic – to notice details. 'Who are you?' he would ask, 'How do I say your name? May I sit down?' His questions, the humility of his approach, are the starting point of accepting that this country, though unfamiliar to him, is known and named, and grants him a place to stand as an outsider, a foreigner.

I first read Lopez when I was twenty-two, in preparation for a three-month trip to Alaska. His book *Arctic Dreams* was a revelation. His poet's eye ranged over zoology, anthropology, environmental science, and he wrote about country and

Indigenous knowledge with respect and delight. His writing was suffused with generosity and reciprocity, and prepared me for the shock of walking on country that reared out of the ground with a force and violence I'd never seen in Australia. The snow-covered peaks were still fantastical and foreign to my eyes, which were trained on flattened plains and ancient, eroded mountains, but Lopez's descriptions of Alaska gave me the imaginative space to begin to see this new landscape.

From Lopez I read Gretel Ehrlich and Annie Dillard, Terry Tempest Williams, and back further to Ralph Waldo Emerson and Henry Thoreau, and this written lineage of transcendental experiences in landscape was a different heritage from our bush ballads of brokenness, of drought-ravaged, desperate country. America's founding myth of manifest destiny did not fit so well in Australia's brutal history, where the falsehood of *terra nullius* silenced our First Nations stories and knowledge and was wielded as a justification for stealing country.

So I'm right to feel the discomfort, right to feel like a thief. I'm also right to bring all of my senses to this country; to ask, who are you? How do I say your name? And may I sit down?

In the morning we visit the source of the Darling River. It's an ancient amphitheatre. We walk out onto a small headland. On one side is the Bogan River and on the other the Barwon River, and where they meet the Darling begins. There are trees here that must be many hundreds of years old. I sit myself against one and watch the martins swoop in and out of the mud nests built high around a burl. This could be the Garden of Eden. We're all silenced by the place. Both the rivers are still empty – they look like death not life, their skeletons are laid bare, nothing covers them. I feel ashamed.

Then we see water moving, but it is flowing upstream, towards us. It's from a creek further down where there has been rain in the catchment and it has flooded into the Darling, which is so empty that the water has pushed back up into it, filling it from below. This makes me want to weep – in sadness, but also in wonder that the river is so close to death. Unnatural things are happening to it.

It's hard to say goodbye, hard to leave this country. My friend gives me some red-tailed black cockatoo feathers to take home. One is from the tail of the female and is striped with thin red bands like a tiger. The male tail feather has a thick and brilliant band of red across it. They are on my desk now, and every time I see them I'm taken back to that powerful place. We stand beside the car and watch as a sea eagle flaps from the river with something gripped in its talons. Then a little mob of white spoonbills, who have been living for months with my friend's flock of guinea fowls, start to spiral up and up like a curl of smoke, until they are so high we can't see them anymore. I stand with my head craned back, my eyes straining. A willie wagtail appears as I open the door of the car. The bird hops along the fence and twitches its tail. He's talking to me and I'm missing the message. I know.

Duty gets me in the car. Duty keeps me there.

We drive south out of the storm-blessed green and into the dry again. Still no relief for so many. When we get back to Coonamble I go for a long walk. I walk until the sun sets and then turn around and retrace my steps in the almost blackness of a winter evening. I have a sudden urge to feel the dirt under my feet, and instead of dismissing this as folly I sit in the middle of the road and take my boots off and then walk carefully until I run out of road. I don't dare walk through the paddocks without boots so I put them on again, climb through the fence and follow the dry creek bed back to the cottage. Inside, there's a fire blazing in the fireplace and the small room is thick with friends. I cook dinner and enjoy being in the kitchen, on the edge, listening as they banter with J. We're leaving tomorrow, heading south to the 'inside country', as my friend calls it. I know J will find it hard to leave, but for different reasons.

I'm more open out here, more hopeful, filled with energy as if the faraway horizon feeds me, hands me ideas and optimism. Part of this is being away from the grind of home, but there's also a layer of belonging that sweeps me with a relief I don't recognise as needing when I'm in Tasmania. It's only when it's there that I realise I have accommodated the sadness of living away from it.

Driving south, we pass swathes of green country followed by strips of barren land on which no rain has fallen. It must be sanity-smashing to see grass on your boundary fence and none in your paddocks.

When we get on the plane in Melbourne we've driven more than three thousand kilometres.

*

Back at the farm, the ewes are all well settled, more settled than us. We're returning to another winter. It hasn't rained while we were gone and the long-term forecast is depressing. The images of those huge river channels empty of water hang over me, but I'm also carrying the flash of hope the country gifted me.

The dogs are mad with energy and I take them for a long walk. I also take a bucket of feed for the horses. Though they've had a round bale of hay and a neighbour checking on them, I've been worried about them in such a tough season. The dogs rumble and wrestle across the paddock as I call the horses. They come galloping; the dust rises from their hooves and their breath makes halos around their heads. They snort and dance, wild for a moment, even Old Will. But then I tip the feed into their bins and each of them blows a sweet breath onto me, a gift, a small welcome home. When they are all still and eating I move from one to the next and rub my hands in their thick winter coats, notice the spreading grey hairs on the two old ones. For a moment, the feeling I've been unable to name, which has travelled with me all of the three thousand kilometres, lifts.

I felt lost.

In returning to the places I've always belonged, to the place where I'm named and known, I still felt lost. The feeling, which I have been unable to pin down, was disorientating. I know I am describing a typical emigrant experience of being caught between two worlds, but there was something more. I leave the horses and set off up the hill, then drop down across the creek and climb up onto the ridge. The dogs crash through the bush and startle an eagle, and the sight of it, though not unusual, jolts me. For a moment I'm not sure where I am. Distance falls away, and light, and I spot the same sea eagle I saw just after dawn on the headwater of the Darling. When I look again I see this eagle has a small bloody body in the grip of its talons, a rabbit perhaps? It flaps to a tree and wedges its meal in a forking branch. Then it watches as I walk away.

We are two weeks off the shortest day of the year and the light doesn't leak from the day anymore; instead it falls with startling swiftness, and I find myself tripping, unable to make out the contours of the earth. I find a sheep track and follow the powdered dust, needing my blood to pump and the movement to free my thinking. I stop trying to see my way and trust my feet to find the path. The track is made by the hooves of sheep walking long distances from where we feed them back to the one remaining waterhole. I drop down the steep bank and stumble over the rocks on the creek bed. Here the creek is only dry stones. I have to believe the water is deep under them.

The dark is rising now, the grey of dusk replaced with crisp black, out of which the skeletons of gums mark my track home. By the time I get there J will have gone to the pub to check his footy tips and discuss our trip with the regulars over a beer. I've lost the corgis, but Dusty, my labrador, who is the one I worry will get on a scent and be gone for days, has stuck with me. She raises her nose to the night air and opens her mouth – I hear her rather than see her tasting all the night animals creeping out. We've had this argument too many times, but I make a soft breathy whistle just to keep her with me. We climb out of the creek bed, walk across the flat, back to where I've left the horse-feed buckets. The horses are still chasing out the last bits of grain in their feed bins. I warm my hands on the coats of my old friends and then keep walking back to the house. I'm acutely aware of my aloneness. It's such a contrast to the busyness of the hours between 5 and 7 pm when the children were small. This peace, this solitude, were what I longed for then. Now I have it and I feel lost.

Is this what I am not understanding? That there are two layers to my displacement? I am on the cusp of freedom, of no longer being defined by the immediate needs of my children, but that freedom brings with it a lack of definition.

Who am I if I am not a mother?

When I get back to the house J has stoked the fire and filled the wood basket before heading out. The house is dark and quiet. The corgis haven't shown up so I switch on the lights, feed Dusty, turn the oven down to keep dinner warm and come through to my desk. It's cold in here. I type with fingerless gloves, a beanie on my head and sheepskin boots on my feet, and even though the fire cracks behind my back I can still see my breath. I want to follow the trace of this thought. How have I become so lost?

Becoming a mother is a sort of trauma, or it was for me. I was instantly transformed, almost against my will. I became fierce with love and the need to protect. My desires were second to A's needs and yet my desire was her. So if I wanted to write a book, or climb a mountain, or ride a horse, I had to steal from myself the time to do it. This identification became stronger when I became my children's only parent, a position underlined again when my own mother died.

So many wonderful people stepped into the vacuum created by these losses. But still my whole being orbited around the needs of those children. I was not, in certain regards, a particularly attentive mother. I let my children watch too much TV. I neglected to listen to them read out loud; I did not enforce the completion of homework. But I heard their heart's desire and tried to make it happen for each of them. I drove C to rugby games and A to show-jumping competitions. I went to running carnivals and swimming carnivals (until they hit high school and then I said enough and never went to another one). I spent my money on their hobbies, on their education. I gave them a love of reading, the knowledge that beauty saves us all, that a swim in cold water or greeting the dawn outside can shift the blackest moments. And I hope I have given them their independence. But now, on the cusp of that independence, with one of them already out in the world and the other one about to leave, I realise I have given so much that I have lost sight of myself.

At all the points of change in my life – my husband dying so young, my mother dying, leaving academia to raise my kids on the farm, moving to Tasmania for love, staying in Tasmania – uppermost has been what will be best for the kids. I've sometimes resented the lack of choice motherhood has forced on me. But now, in this fluid in-between space, when I see the familiar cloak of my mothering needs to be laid down for a lighter garment, as I shift into this next phase, I feel tired.

Once, J told me he was ploughing a paddock, going round and round, when he noticed two wedge-tailed eagles bashing up a young eagle. He said it was so brutal he thought they were going to kill it. He rang the eagle refuge on the outskirts of Hobart (you have a lot of time when you are going around and around a big paddock) and the woman he spoke to told him it was probably the parents forcing the chick to leave their territory. Eagles must raise their chick to independence: if a young one hangs around, the parents make life so unpleasant that it is forced to leave, or die.

I think perhaps I am the opposite of those eagle parents. I'm too eager for C to come home on the weekends from school, too eager to enjoy his company, too aware that in the shortest time he will be leaving home. The eagles force their young to leave so they will find a mate. They have another chick to take care of. The cycle of their parenting is fast. Perhaps that's it, too: this letting-go feels too fast after all those early years when the hours of the days crawled, where weeks seemed impossibly long, where the sheer exhaustion of looking after two small children made it impossible – dangerous, even – to think of a time when there was more freedom. From that sagging time to this. I am not ready, yet it's here.

Who will I be after C goes? How are we changed once the anchor of the children's needs is lifted and we're free to put ours first? Perhaps I'll have more time to write. I certainly will have more money. I think back to my teenage self, the girl who was obsessed with horses, whose only desire was to ride every day. I wonder how I shut that down so hard; I wonder if I can let it rise up again; I wonder if reclaiming something I used to love is a way into this next stage, or is it just a circling back to another sort of familiarity?

There's a thump at the back door. The corgis are back. I shut my computer and let the world of hungry dogs and domestic chores swallow me.

There's just one more thing to tell you about the swallows. It is our winter routine to watch TV and eat our dinner in front of the open fire. The fire is mostly for me. If J's on his own he pulls an ancient bar heater up to his chair and hunches over its soulless warmth. From the kitchen, where I am making a winter salad of chopped kale, tough beetroot leaves and parsley, which is all that has survived the dry season, I see him switching on the veranda light as he fetches wood from the shed. The swallows, fluffed up and warm against winter's chill, swoop with a chirp over his head and perch in the cold on the far end of the veranda. When I bring my tray in for dinner the fire is blazing and the veranda light is still on. It makes me smile. Woe betide anyone who leaves the light on in the room when they are not in it – they will be lectured. But for two swallows to find their way back to their warm nest, the light is left on. By winter's end the swallows simply watch J as he gets his load of wood from beneath their perch.

And in this way we all carry on.

There, on a bloodied ewe, is an eagle. I get out to open the gate and the bird sees me. It lowers its head, spreads its wings but does not take off. It's a young sea eagle, its chest feathers are not yet starched to the crisp white of a mature bird, and it's reluctant to leave its breakfast. We drive towards it and, intimidated at last, it beats its wings until the air fills under them and then, for a moment, it hovers, before turning clumsily to roost in the limb of a dead tree. We pull up beside the ewe expecting the worst. But the ewe has been lucky. The eagle has not been feeding on her, but on her half-born lamb.

Our arrival has caused the rest of the mob to drift away, except for a confused day-old lamb who has lost its mother and is sticking close to the cast ewe. The bloodied ewe, who has given herself over to death, doesn't move as I approach. Her exposed udder has been robbed, the waxy seal that forms over an expectant mother's teats is gone and her bag is soft on the side the opportunistic lamb has sucked. I mutter to the lamb to go and find its real mother. It doesn't move so I make myself an eagle. I spread my arms and flap at it to drive it away from the cast ewe and towards the mob, where its mother is most certainly. It scampers away from me then stops, uncertain, looking back to the bloodied ewe. I signal for J to turn the ute off. The world falls silent. We forget how loud, how intrusive we are. The lamb bleats again and there at the back of the mob is a ewe turning. She calls loudly to the lamb, who, like a spring released runs hard towards her.

In the quiet J pulls the mangled carcass of the half-born lamb from the ewe and we load her onto the ute. It's undignified but effective. I take the hind legs and J the front legs and we swing her up and onto the tray and prop her, still cast, all four legs in the air. She is in a fugue state, still thinks she is going to die. But she's whole, she's alive and when I get her back to the yards she will wake from her stupor. She will be thirsty and I'll give her a drink. She'll be hungry and I'll give her something to eat. She will search for a lamb and I'll give her one of those, too.

The air is sharp with the tang of birth and death.

A FRIEND OF MINE HAS AN ELEPHANT MEMORY. Her recall is astounding: people's faces, dates, conversations. Her mind is a well-ordered filing system. She will amaze those around her with details of conversations, of weather and circumstance, clothing even. It's like she flicks an index in her head and up pops the moment, as rich or barren as its birth. She can remember what we wore as sixteen-year-olds to a party in a paddock when we got drunk and both kissed a boy. She can remember who was at my older brother's eighteenth birthday party, when I can't even remember we had one for him. I envy her. My impulse is towards erasure, to close my mind to what has happened and move on.

After the birth of my daughter, I walked beside my husband as he pushed along the hospital corridor the tiny clear cot in which she lay, taking her from the delivery room to the maternity ward (in the same hospital where, five years later, my husband would scale a wall in the exercise yard of the secure psychiatric ward, make his way to the cliffs close by and fall to his death). I was determined to walk. The midwives had offered me a wheelchair, but I thought, how odd, I'm not sick, my baby has been born, I did that, and now you offer me a wheelchair? I needed to walk. I needed to get back into my body, feel the sensation of one foot in front of the other, let my feet feel my body's lesser weight. For I'd been transformed. Lit by pain I could have never imagined, my body had shifted into something else. In that place of birthing, the moment of becoming a mother, I was unrecognisable to myself. But walking. The familiar swinging – one leg then the other – returned me and I became once more known. The corridor felt potent. The midwife, whose Irish lilt had called me forward through the birth, paused with us on its edge. This is a magic space, she said. On one side all the women are never having another baby, and on the other, all the women forget. Not instantly, but collectively, slowly then faster, until we appear back in the delivery suite to make the same promises. Our bodies know it the second time around. The adjustment is no less brutal. But it is not so shocking.

The description of pain is not an easy thing. Here, on the quiet of the page, I can try to pin it more definitively, but out there, in the living, it's almost impossible. Doctors use a scale. How much does it hurt? But what can the person who is in pain say?

*

The creek is now so dry the sheep are using it like a highway to move around the farm. Where there should be deep impassable holes, there are now only shrunken shallow pools. Where there is water, it smells of desperation. The creek is too low to irrigate the garden and we are holding our breath for a decent rain before the winter really settles in. On my walks I keep finding small mobs of twenty or thirty sheep in places they shouldn't be. Merinos like to mob up in big groups. These breakaways show how hard the season is. There are weaned lambs back with the ewes. There are other ewes who have come down off the hill, then worked their way up the creek and joined a big mob of lambs on the eaten-out crop of rape, where even the unpalatable woody stalks have been chewed to a nub. When I look closely I see some plants have the tiniest leaves of hopeful green shooting from the woody stalks. It must be these the sheep are coming back for. They have learnt that fences have weak points, that there is a world on the other side and with persistent application they will find a way to it. I wonder how we will contain this generation of rule-breakers when the drought finally ends.

Drought is catastrophic, life-altering, all-consuming. Hungry animals and cracked bare earth, empty creek beds, dry dams and dirty, stagnant shrinking puddles. Drought also brings an ever-spiralling financial pressure. Do we continue to buy thousands of dollars' worth of feed or do we decide we cannot take on more debt and sell our precious breeding stock? Do we take shortcuts, buy less feed, gamble on a shower of rain and then watch in despair as sheep die and the rain doesn't come and the feed is more expensive still? The financial uncertainty, the mounting debt, the hungry animals make sleep difficult.

I remember the ending of other droughts. The transition from despair to relief. When showers sweep down over the hills, falling every day like a benediction, when the creek flows with clear water, when the country is thick with clover and storybook green, I think, surely, surely the dry couldn't happen again. Remembering is an act of savagery, of self-mutilation, and my mind wants to shield me from it but, like childbirth, like death, the mark is always there.

After my father died, my brother and I were left with the detritus of his life. His partner shipped it to our respective homes. Indiscriminately. The boxes sent to me sat in the front room of the old manager's cottage for nearly two years. I could not deal with them. When I finally opened them, there was my father. Photo after photo, his politician smile plastered on. Also, every letter he had ever written, or so it felt. His desktop swept into a box: catalogues, White Pages, junk mail mixed with photographs of him meeting the Pope, Mao Zedong, various American presidents, dignitaries from Papua New Guinea, India, Russia. My younger brother, with less room, and (characteristically) better organisation, dealt with his boxes sooner.

It is not unusual to be left an orphan in middle age. But the orphan feeling, after the raw grief of each of my parents' death had passed, was an unexpected emotion. Perhaps it was heightened by the responsibility we felt (and still feel) towards our older brother.

Sorting through my father's papers was a task I would have delayed indefinitely had the drought not forced us to diversify and turn the cottage into farm-stay accommodation. I asked J if he could bring me down a 44-gallon drum and put it outside the cottage. In the drum I lit a fire. Then I dragged each box out and dropped the papers into the flames. It took three days. I handled every one. I'd read snatches from a letter, then throw it in the fire. I didn't burn them all. The ones I kept had a glow to them, they wouldn't leave my hand, they were easy to choose. I can't remember how many boxes there were. Many were soaked with rat piss and inside them were pages chewed from years of storage. Others were full of dinner menus from state banquets, notepaper from famous hotels: lacking any context, I burnt them. By the end, the drum was full of ash and as the wind blew, the ash would swirl into the sky, the tiny pieces of paper returning eventually to the earth. I should have buried them, returned the carbon to the ground and let the pages and words dissolve, given them to the worms to chew on, but I needed the catharsis of flame.

I took the thin bundle of papers that glowed and placed them in a sandalwood box, with my mother's and my husband's. When you open the lid of that box, it doesn't smell like death, it smells like memory.

Wedge-tailed eagle, *Aquila audax*. 90 cm–1.1 m; span 2.8 m.
Female larger.
Huge, dark eagle with
whiteish beak, long, closely feathered legs
and long, diamond-shaped tail;
male blacker than female.
Old adults are
mostly black, with varying degrees of chestnut nape; tawny band
across wing.
Flies with easy, powerful wingbeats and
soars
in majestic circles, large tail prominent;
wings noticeably upswept.
Voice: feeble, high-pitched *pseet-you, pseet-you*;
screams in aggressive encounters.
Nest: huge;
of sticks, lined with fresh eucalyptus leaves; in fork or limb, often
high.
Eggs: 1–3,
whiteish, blotched buffish, spotted or streaked red-brown and
lavender.
Many nests produce only one fledgling as
stronger young frequently
kill and eat smaller siblings.

I'M LATE FOR MY WALK. The days are short. Jobs crash into each other, nothing is finished. But I scrape and scrabble my way out the door and over the hill. I walk with my back to the house and sheds, facing west towards the sun setting while the light turns golden and long. Once I am over the crest, the sound of barking dogs and the looping calls of black cockatoos fall away. Into the quiet country the air tastes different and the scent of fire stoked is forgotten. I pass a prickly box tree, its bark hanging in strips, savaged by a stag rubbing the velvet from his antlers. I pick my way down the stony track to the creek crossing.

The dogs are scattered. They are high on the scent of roo and possum. I walk away from the creek and up onto the rocky ridge, moving fast, trying to outpace the falling sun. After sitting at my desk all day, I want the spurt of blood, the pound of heart, so I put my head down and thunder up the hill. Perhaps I'm deafened by the swish of life through me, or blinded by the dazzle of low rays, but I don't see the eagle until I'm almost on top of it. It rears up and thumps the air and I'm grazed by its fierceness. My dogs dash at it, all bravado and fear. I yell and they hush.

And so we stand. Meet in the gloaming.

It's huge. Its head reaches my hip and its legs are like feathered totem poles impossibly armed with claws like scythes. Its beak is a wicked hook and it hisses its wildness at me.

It's hurt. Otherwise it would be gone. Never have I been so close to an eagle not caged. I've startled them feeding on sheep, but they take off like military planes from an aircraft carrier – *thump, thump, thump*; ponderously they rise till they receive the grace of air, bank away and are gone. I've peered at one recovering in a chook pen after being hit by a truck, but I've never seen one like this. Its presence is tightening the air and I don't know what to do. This bird does not want to be here. It does not want me to see it. It wants to be high, hanging, far above. I step back, circle away and crouch down. I say, I see you, but I will not look.

There's a dead sheep further up the hill. It's perhaps why the eagle is still alive. I sit with the stench of death and watch the bird. It knows I'm watching, but it doesn't hide. When I call J he doesn't answer, last I saw him he was lying on his back in the dirt wrestling with a broken plough. I leave a message – 'I've found an injured eagle,' I say. 'I'm not sure what to do, call me when you get this.' The bird (can I call it this?) stares so I am small. I whistle the dogs and keep walking to where it can't see me, then I sit on a tussock of grass and type into the YouTube browser of my phone 'how to catch an eagle'.

Tasmanian wedge-tailed eagles are endangered. There are around a hundred breeding pairs left. They are a subspecies of the more common wedgetail that are shot by farmers on the mainland, and here, too. And I almost understand. I've seen an eagle feeding on a cast ewe, the ewe's kicks feeble under the strength of the eagle's talons and its hooked beak.

I remember one ewe.

We were in the middle of lambing. We'd had little trouble from one mob of about four hundred ewes in the paddock called Bridge Flat (because there's a bridge in it). They were easy to see with binoculars from the hill above the paddock, but this day we drove in to check the banks of the creeklet that trickles its way to the sea. It was here, just below the lip of the creek, that we found a ewe cast. The ground was swept bare and scarred by her struggles. Her head was stripped of wool and flesh on one side. She had no eye, no ear, the faintest outline of flesh on her jaw, you could see her teeth. I gasped – she can't be alive – but she was and I panicked at her suffering and begged J to end it with a quick slash of his knife to her throat. I couldn't look at her. He went over to her and she kicked and kicked. She wants to live, he said, and he picked her up and put her on the back of the ute. We took her to the yards, gave her water and hay, pumped her full of penicillin and she stood bloody, half-faced and defiantly alive. It was an eagle who'd fed on her. No crow could do that much damage.

I'm still thinking about her when my phone rings.

I can hear exasperation bite into J's words. He's had a bad day. Broken discs on the plough have delayed him getting a crop in and he is battling to get it finished before a predicted rain (it never came). 'A wedgie,' he says and I hear his questioning lilt. He manages to stop himself outright asking if I'm sure and, god bless him, puts down his tools and asks me where I am. He'll be there in ten minutes.

When he arrives he's on the phone to the raptor rescue man, who lives south of Hobart. I hear J say, 'Yes, mate, it's definitely a wedgetail.' Still the man makes him send a photograph. We wait for the reply in the sound of his phone's ping. 'You're right,' the man says. 'A wedgie. You'll have to catch it.' He explains how.

If the eagle makes for the thick scrub by the creek, it will be impossible to reach, so I scamper like a sheepdog and get round it to push it out onto rocky, open ground. The raptor man told us we must surround the eagle until it is so threatened it flips onto its back and bares its talons at us, at which point we are to bundle it up in something. I look at the great floating bulk of the creature. It strains for the open space above as we close in; it hops and flaps, becomes more desperate, less wild – and then we are upon it. Sure enough, it flips on its back and its talons glint in the setting sun. J throws a coat over it and pounces. He bundles it up until only its head is free. It opens its mouth but no sound comes.

J carries the bird back to the ute, its anger a pulse. When we get back to the sheds he finds a 1-tonne bag we use to cart sheep feed and I line it with an old horse rug. We push the huge bird into it and watch as it rights itself and realises it is not to be killed. We leave it in the quiet, the night air funnelled to it through the loosely gathered top. Tomorrow J will take it to town to meet the raptor rescue man. Now, he heads back to wrestling with the tractor and I walk home. Winter's hoary breath settles on my shoulders.

At the house I push fresh wood into the belly of the fire, fill the wood basket and turn on the oven. We live between the domestic and the wild, linked by nature and, it seems, either protecting it, trading with it, or using it for our own means. It's a constant seesaw of compromise. This life for that. This lamb raised for wool, that one for meat. This eagle trapped by us, in the hope it will survive. That ewe attacked by an eagle, unable to be saved. I think of sheep tracks across an open paddock; they appear as an invitation, a random path, but they never are. And I think of my feet making new tracks, crisscrossing this place. Perhaps my movements are likewise more intentional than I can see, and if I keep myself open, keep watching, I'll make my peace with the choices I've made.

This morning we checked a big paddock with good shelter from the bush pressing down onto its edges. There's plenty of room for a ewe to lamb in private, but the bush also offers protection for predators. Up the top of the paddock, on a bank spotted with bracken, is a ewe blackened by crows. There must be twenty of the birds swarming over her, making her dance with their plucking. They are so bold they flap lazily off only as we drive up. C, who's home on school holidays, hops out. Mercifully, the ewe is dead. I let myself believe that happened before the crows found her. We all spread out looking for a lamb. After twenty minutes we give up. There's a dead lamb further down the hill; it might be hers. J drives over to a pile of timber and I'm grateful for C's muscle as he throws the ewe's body on. From the top of the ute he sees another ewe who has been attacked. She has lost both her eyes to the crows and her back end has been savaged. She is still alive. J slits her throat and she goes on the timber pile too. I feel dulled by the brutality. Then I see her lamb. It's sheltered beneath a clump of tussock and hidden from the crows.

It's not until I get back to the house and look at the lamb properly that I realise how tiny it is. It's too weak to suck, but I pour some colostrum down its throat and give it a few minutes wrapped up by the fire. The colostrum is a magic potion. When I pick the lamb up again and put the teat in its mouth, it sucks feebly. I'll feed it again in a few hours and it will be stronger still. The instinct to suck, lost in the trauma of its birth, grows back in the dark and quiet, and I think sometimes for the young to live, the mother must die.

WHEN MY ALARM GOES OFF I lie buried beneath flannel sheets, doona and the handspun wool rug my aunt made and dread the moment I must get out of bed. The air will bite. My clothes will be stiff with cold. There is an inevitable and unavoidable level of discomfort ahead. Then I'm up. I throw on my clothes, beanie and fingerless gloves, shove my feet in thick woollen socks and my sheepskin boots.

In the courtyard I open the wood stove, which burns all winter. The cold rushes onto the coals and they flare in defiance. With a heavy copper dustpan, I steal some coals to light my study fire. The copper glows and warms. There is something about carrying the glowing coals through the dark of the house that connects me to every woman who has carried hot coals to start fires, boil water, cook a meal. The copper becomes soft and tender in my hand as the heat brings it to life. I empty the coals over pine cones and in moments a fire cracks and pops and the room is full of dancing shadows.

Outside, the trees creak with frost and the dark is absolute. The owl and possum, wallaby and wombat, devil and potoroo are all heading back to their holes before the first leak of light rises over a frozen world.

My mother used to greet each day before the rest of the world stirred. She'd rise in the dark and seek renewal in the quiet. She's been dead fifteen years now and her absence has grown more familiar than the ache of her loss. In the time after she died, I felt her leaving as fatigue in my arms, as a tightness in my throat where words caught. Then for years I got used to her not being here. I ceased to want her. Or, I ceased to allow myself to want her.

It helped that I didn't need her in those fundamental ways I had as a young, single mother; in fact, chances are that if she were alive, I would be adjusting to a new role of caring for her. I look at eighty-year-old women for clues as to who my mother would have become, what she would have looked like, how she would have settled into herself as a grandmother, what passions she would have had time to develop. When my mother's younger sister comes to stay, she brings my mother's presence with her. It's just a hint, like a lingering scent. I watch as my aunt slows down time. She has the gift of peace. Her hands are rarely still, but she's never in a hurry.

Perhaps it is my mother I mimic in rising in the still time of early morning, when the day bristles with possibility but has not yet started. I've reached a lull in my mothering, or a gentler place, a place to float and let the tide carry me. I have a sense of being on the cusp of something new, while the memory of all that has come before is sitting below my skin. I need to lay my weapons down. I need to stand back and watch my children leave. How, though. How do I do this? In this season of want, this dry time, when we wait with pinched desperation for rain, I realise I'm seeking my mother for the answers.

Later, I walk out into the frost. The cold sings in my toes and fingers as I stride up the hill and breathe crystalline air deep into me. The horses stand side-on to the morning sun. The hair on their necks opens to let the warmth onto their skin and their breath hangs like a bouquet beneath their noses. I throw them some hay and warm my hands under the rug of the grey pony as he noses through the hay looking for the sweet, seeded heads of summer grasses. My black dog charges out of the bracken, her coat flecked with the jewels of frost and her pink tongue lapping at the frozen air.

We head away from the sheds, the tall pine trees and the curling smoke of the chimneys, out into the frozen world. In my pocket is a notebook and pen. It's a different sort of walking I'm doing.

I'm sick of rushing. I used to run in the mornings because I could cover twice the distance in half the time. Forty minutes, I'd say to myself as I strapped on my watch, did my shoelaces up and sprinted out the door – twenty minutes out, twenty minutes back, and that's exercise ticked off for the day. I would notice the creak of frost in the trees, the crystals on the gate posts and the first sting of cold on my fingers, but soon I'd be swept into the runner's meditation of lung burn and heart pump. I liked the buzz and fizz of moving through the world fast. Running is efficient, I'd be back and into the day and rush and push and bustle and fuss. Now I want something different.

Up the hill we walk, and the dogs fan out around me. I listen as our arrival is noticed. Three crows – though actually they are forest ravens – high in the limbs of a dead eucalypt call an alarm. Off to my right is a mob of last year's lambs. They are used to the sight of me walking, but still I hear the snort of one sounding the alarm. I've heard a ewe snort like this and seen her lamb drop straight to the ground, instantly motionless. These older lambs move to bunch up, then realise it's me and watch me walk by. Some of them drop their heads to keep grazing, though the ground cover is so short I wonder how they are finding a feed. The scent of wood smoke is gone and I'm away from the yards pressing deeper into this world. A gang of noisy miners screeches at me from a thick stand of wattle and she-oak, and I look to see what they are carrying on about. A young stag, still in velvet, plunges through the undergrowth. He leaps the muddy bog where the creek should run and charges up the steep rocks on the other side. I whistle and my bejewelled black dog comes back. The corgis, golden in the white morning, race in hopeless pursuit. I see the stag crest the ridge and disappear. The corgis will give up and find me soon enough.

The black dog and I cross ploughed ground that's still hard with frost and enter the bush, the secret heart of the farm. Here, all the things come to hide, to sleep in burrows through the day and push out to graze the pasture at night. I follow a trail made by the soft feet of wallaby and wombat through the bracken. By now trees are starting to drip as the world warms. I reach a small clearing, sit on a log in a pale pool of spilling sun and wait for the dogs to find me. A family of magpies is singing. The sound is so pure it almost hurts. I've broken into their world and I wait for it to shuffle itself around me. I've brought nothing with me save my notebook and pen.

A long time ago I would have written a prayer in the notebook. But now I do not believe in God. Or I do not believe in the god my mother did. Her god was of Billy Graham crusades, of blind people seeing, of the crippled walking and (killer hook), the mute speaking. Her god was the god of the journey, of the mysterious making and remaking of self under the burdens sent to test and strengthen her. Her god punished and rescued, according to her level of faith. Her god saved her, and perhaps he (and he was most definitely a he) saved us too. That's the god I do not believe in anymore.

I am not attacking or criticising my mother's beliefs. I'm trying to understand the woman she was and the woman she became. My mother *had* to believe otherwise she would have left my brother, perhaps us, definitely my father (though she did eventually do this shortly before her death). Her belief kept her from madness. It rescued her and it tethered her.

My faith – though with the gift of hindsight I think it was my mother's faith imprinted onto me – washed off slowly and then in a great rush after my husband died. When my mother died, I laid down my desire to believe in anything. And I stayed like that for a long time. It was enough for me to get through the day.

Sitting on the log, my notebook blank, I think I'm looking again for a god. My mother searched for answers to impossible questions in her Bible each morning. There, she would find the metaphor she needed to get through another day. Even after I'd left home she would tell me the stories of her comfort. I wouldn't listen. And now this new need for her, this rising up of want on the other end of my own mothering, surprises me. I'm shocked, embarrassed even. I'm middle-aged. Surely this is not the time to need your mother so urgently. Yet I am not doing well. I am not calmly accepting of this season of my life. In fact, I'm unravelling, spinning away from the axis of my children's needs, which has kept me rooted to the present. With the urgency they elicited gone, I am exposed.

Perhaps finding some sense of continuity, of connection in the simple making and breaking of every day, is enough. The thing is, to see myself as part of this cycle means I must make my peace with letting my children go, it means I must make my peace with death.

I thought I had grieved for my mother, I thought I had learnt to let my sorrow move through me lightly, to stop in the moments it arrived, let it rest on me and then continue on my way. And I have grieved, I have managed to live with her absence, but what this season is showing me is that there is a deeper grief I haven't understood and the ache of seeing it is dangerous.

Once, when I attended an online writing workshop, the teacher asked us to imagine our future selves. It was at the end of four days of intense writing and she was seeking to give us tools to keep going after her encouraging presence disappeared. She asked us to imagine this older person and to figuratively and literally ask them for wisdom and insight into our writing. 'Think of it as time travel,' she said, 'and ask what it is you need to know.' The task was uncomfortable. I could not imagine myself old. Could not imagine myself past the age my mother was when she died. Could not ask my older self for advice because, I realised, she was not there.

Afterwards, I went and stood in front of a mirror. Here is the evidence of my ageing: my skin is soft and full of wrinkles. I see my mother, but I also see me. I see lines of stress and laughter. A smile. I touch my skin and feel just there, under my fingertips, my mother's wisdom, her peace, her optimism. She was like a cave out of which I crept into the world, but always knowing she was waiting there as shelter. I remember my ten-year-old self weeping with rage and frustration that I had to return to school, to the city from the farm. For the previous six weeks I had abandoned my family and lived in a world full of horses and dogs and sheep and birds. The night we returned, I lay in bed, inconsolable. My mother came to say goodnight. I sobbed about a whole term of school to get through before I could go back again. My mother bent herself to my pain, and then a thought struck her and she left me to fetch a pen and paper. On it she drew a graph of my life. She made me watch and showed me the span of that life, the infinite possibilities. She wrote on the paper all the things I loved: riding, working with sheep and dogs, raising chooks, gardening, watching birds. Then she wrote down all the things I hated: school, the city, concrete gutters, footpaths and tiny neat gardens, my brother. She showed me how small the time was in my life during which I had to go to school, when I could not do what I wanted. She punctuated this time with visits to the farm, little holidays, and when she drew it all out, the stretch of life did feel full of possibilities. I felt empowered to survive what was before me.

What I need now is another map. But she is not here to draw it.

Instead, I look in the mirror, seeking the older woman ahead of me. The older woman says, press into age, learn your wrinkles like you learnt your growing breasts and pregnant body.

Sitting on the log in this frosty morning, my notebook blank, I realise I've a new version of my mother's map and from it she dares me to imagine myself old.

The chiding of a family of superb blue wrens announces the dogs as they push through the bracken, their pink tongues bright in the still morning, panting their delight at tracking me down. We set off for home. The morning is so still I can hear the tractor rumbling up the lane. We're in Dry Creek and there's a big mob of ewes. They camp in the shelter of bracken and gorse that edges the creek. I imagine their thermal mass on a morning like this. The valley is white with frost, but their collective bodies form a single beating swell of heat. At the sound of the tractor they move as one up the paddock to wait at the double gates. During lambing they will cease to be a single mob and split into hundreds of individual stories. A small percentage of them will have trouble lambing, and I know that this year is going to be worse because there is no feed on the ground and no water in the waterholes or creek. Those who have trouble will cease to be anonymous, they will become known, even if the only person who knows them is me. We are both, the ewe and I, changed by the knowing.

I open the gate for the tractor and head across the flat to walk up the creek. On the way back there is a patch of gorse that was cleared by a bulldozer last summer. J must have lit it last night. All that's left is a pile of ash ringed by a few gnarled limbs that must have fallen out of the blaze. In the gentle sun the centre of the ash still smokes. I haul the outer ring of tangled roots, trunks and dead needles and place them over the smoking ash. Kneeling, I bend and blow and a flame leaps onto the hint of oil in the dried needles. It flickers then flares. I pile the blaze with more wood. The heat is fierce and licks my face so I turn away. Ash shadows my knees and I realise I have knelt as if to pray.

Yellow-tailed black cockatoo, *Calyptorhynchus funereus*, 55–65 cm.
Large black cockatoo with pale feather margins, and large pale-
yellow panels in long tail.
Male: bill blackish; eye ring reddish; dull yellow spot
on ear coverts.
Female: bill whitish; eye ring grey; bright yellow spot
on ear coverts,
yellow tail panels
etched brown.
Pairs, family trios; autumn to winter in flocks of hundreds.
Tears bark from eucalyptus and wattle exposing
'white grubs'.
Flocks feed on ground and in foliage on seed capsules of hakeas,
banksias,
exotic pines.
Flight *buoyant* with slow,
deep wingbeats.
Demonstrative on wing, wheeling, spreading,
flashing yellow tail panels,
Voice: weird, far-carrying, squealing
why-lay or *wee-lar*, much conversational chuckling and
giggling from flocks in flight.
Harsh screeches in alarm; grinding, begging sounds from young.
Nest: on decayed debris, in large tree hollow, usually high.
Eggs: 1–2; white, oval;
usually only one offspring
survives.

They wheel overhead, two, three, four, then a dozen or more arrive on the far edge of daylight as the western horizon turns pink, then orange, then red. They sit in the pine trees and crack the hard shell of the cones for the sweet nut inside, then drop the cones in a shower, each a small hand grenade. They bob from the trees like the plumes worn by black horses. One giggles and the others pluck at my thoughts and toss them gleefully to each other and I wait for the freefall of their sudden departure. They used to have a reputation for bringing rain. I don't believe this anymore, but I welcome them because of their beauty, the sighing wonder of their flight.

Other times they come to feast on wattle grubs. They gather on the hill above the yards where the wattles grow in thickets. It's like a bar. The birds strut and preen, pull strips of bark off the wattle branches. They are like schoolchildren wrestling. Their beaks crack open the edge of the trees and the sound ripples like frost thawing.

Words that are useful to know

SHEEP GRAZIER ALERT

A warning for sheep graziers for Midlands, Upper Derwent Valley and South East forecast districts. 'Sheep graziers are warned that cold temperatures, showers and strong westerly winds are expected. There is a risk of losses of lambs and sheep exposed in these conditions.'

MY YOUNGER BROTHER AND I talk on the phone a few times a week. His life in Sydney working for an international company, juggling time zones and egos, while living in an inner-city suburb with two young children, is different from the rhythm of my days. We often talk while he's taking his Scottish terrier, Bob, for a walk along the banks of the Cooks River. It's his little slice of wildness. Our conversations are dotted with asides to our four-legged companions. We talk about what we're reading, what we're listening to, we talk about the kids and about our own childhood. One day he told me that his wife, a social worker, observed that children are more resilient if they have a story to fit their trauma around. A child with a story has something to stand within, even when the reality of their world is crumbling.

In the July of my daughter's eighth year, two years after her father died and six months after her grandmother died,

I bought her a horse. I had just left my job as a lecturer at Sydney University and moved back to the farm where my mother grew up. Buying the horse felt reckless – and not in a wild and exuberant sort of way, but out of desperation to give this child something bigger than the emotions she was feeling. It was financial madness and another big responsibility at a time in my life when I was only just coping with an out-of-control two-year-old and a highly anxious eight-year-old. But my gut was telling me that, as scary as it was, what my daughter needed was a story to stand within.

A friend's father, a fine horseman, told me he'd found a horse that might suit us. The thirteen-year-old of unknown heritage had been a drover's horse and, more recently, had some pony-club experience. We visited the horse, all of us, my friend, her father, my son and my daughter, who seemed shocked that such a creature could be hers.

Up until this moment my daughter had only experienced actual horses on special occasions. The rest was in her head. She had gone riding for her birthday, forty-five expensive minutes that I know did not measure up to her vivid anticipation, and my friend's mum had borrowed a very old pony when we stayed with them one holiday so my daughter could help look after it. The kindness of this still makes me smile. I have a photograph of the two of them washing that old pony's tail. The photo shows A with a look of just-contained happiness, brush in one hand, the other buried in the pony's thick white winter coat.

*

The thought that an actual horse could come to live with us was too big for her to hold.

He was saddled and bridled when we arrived. 'What's his name?' my daughter asked. His name was Will. Will was a bright chestnut with a white blaze, which started with declarative boldness and petered out to a trickle as it got to the end of his nose. He was not good-looking. His head was too big, his ears too small, his rump enormous and his neck quite short, but he claimed the ground he stood on and looked at us with calm interest. I was suddenly nervous, so my friend rode him before I did. He trotted and cantered obediently, picked up his correct leads and stopped when asked. Then my daughter climbed on. She was a small child and he was quite a big horse. She looked tiny on his back. I didn't know if I was ready for this to happen. She was less than a beginner, had been on a horse maybe twice or three times, but she sat ramrod straight on his back and her inability to rise to the trot or do more than suggest where she might like him to go did not faze him a bit. In fact, he went more kindly for her than he did for my friend or me.

I bought him. My friend's mum helped and also one of my mother's best friends. These women wanted to bring something positive back into my shattered life. But I was terrified. I lay awake that night questioning myself, rehearsing different scenarios of how this could go wrong. If you had asked me then why I was buying a horse I would have told you it was to teach my daughter resilience and independence, to give her a taste of being able to do something bigger than her small self, and those reasons were good reasons and true. What I didn't know, what I couldn't know, was that this horse would not just rescue my daughter, he would rescue me too. In buying him I was giving my kids a story. On his broad back they learnt to jump logs, chase cows and muster sheep. In the summer they'd ride him bareback down to the mulberry tree so they could stand, balanced precariously on his back to reach the high branches. They'd come home with their hands and faces stained purple. In winter I'd boil barley on the stove to add to his feed. It would fill the kitchen with an earthy essence as it swelled and softened. I'd carry the cooling pot up to the stable, mix it with freshly cut lucerne chaff and pour it into his feed bin. Then I'd lean my head against his neck and listen to the primordial crunch of his jaws. Down in the cottage the kids were asleep, and I'd sit for a moment and know a simple, deep peace.

That was sixteen years ago.

This week, this cold bleak week, Will has suddenly and dramatically lost weight. He has been running with my daughter's old thoroughbred mare and her filly. The paddock they live in is beautiful. It's an open flat of chocolate soil with two creeks through it, the shelter of a big hill at one end and at the other a thick tangle of bush that has pockets warmer than most stables. So far I've managed to keep them all looking well despite the drought. I've been feeding them a mix of rolled barley and lucerne chaff and a few biscuits of sweet grass hay every evening for months. They are always lined up at the fence waiting for me. The two old ones have canvas rugs lined with felted wool and I throw these over them as the light fades. The young one has a coat as thick as a bear and more than enough vigour to cope with the cold.

I ring the vet when I get home. She says she will be coming up the coast at the end of the week and I ask her to drop in.

The next day is bitter. There are sheep graziers' warnings on the radio. I fetch an extra woollen rug to put on Will. On the walk down to the paddock I'm pummelled by the wind, leaves fly past me in the air and branches creak ominously. Will is still bright. He nickers when he sees me. But he's not interested in his feed. In all the years he's lived with us he has never been uninterested in his feed. The wind is building in the west, the clouds are dark and angry. I have a sudden premonition. He is going to die. I can't say those words in a sentence. I argue with myself about taking him up to the stable. He hates the stable and it would stress him to be separated from his girls. I put my hand on his neck and ask him what he wants. He tells me to leave him. The clarity of this rocks me. I hold his heavy jug-head in my arms.

I'm sorry, I say. Thank you, I say, and stroke his white blaze, rub his eye. He leans into me, and I am thick with loss.

How do I let him go? I could load him onto the float, rush him to Hobart. Useless, useless. Pain piled on pain. To do so would be not listening to him. To do so would be all about me and not about Will.

In the last crack of light, in the dead of winter's heart, I say goodbye and walk back up the hill. The wind sends arrows of bark into my back. The huge radiata pines rain their needles on my head. It's a Saturday night and C is home. I don't want to tell him that Will is sick. I don't want to tell J either. Both of them will want to do something, fix it, try to save him. And I can't face putting into words my decision to leave him down in the paddock. I just know it is the right thing. I don't have any peace about it, though, so it feels too hard to explain, too hard to defend.

It's so cold outside that the house is warm. A huge fire is blazing in the living room. The courtyard fire glows red. The wind whistles and licks, looking for weakness. I make pizza for dinner, spend ten minutes kneading the dough and feel certainty grow that I've done the right thing. The dough rises by the fire and then C and I stand on either side of the kitchen bench and he shapes it into a pizza and I chop garlic and onion. He's telling me about his week at school, I'm asking him questions, but I'm a long way away. We eat pizza in front of the fire. Rain lashes the windows, but it's only scudding sleet showers, they will barely register in the gauge, and the wind is so strong I wonder whether the drops will even reach the ground.

When it is time for bed I can't sleep. This house has weathered nearly two hundred years of winter storms, which usually comforts me, but tonight I lie awake tortured by my decision to leave Will be.

About midnight I move to the bed in my study. I'm stiff with tension. Nailed to the mattress. I feel close to madness. My jaw aches. I try to reason my way through the dark hours but as soon as I slip towards sleep terror takes over again and wakes me. I can't move. I don't want to get up and turn on the light, read a book, distract myself. I doze. At 4.30 I start wide awake.

He's gone. I felt him go. I lie quietly and dread the dawn, but the suffering is over.

When light comes, I leave the house. It's terribly cold but the wind has dropped. The mares must have heard the back door bang because they call to me to tell me something is wrong. The sky is clean after the storm. Everything looks like it has been rinsed. Leaves glisten, the earth is scented with a little moisture. Up on the hill I see a mob of ewes grazing in blessed stillness. I know what I'm going to see but it's still a shock when I crest the hill and there's no bright chestnut horse with his squiggle blaze. I pour the mares some oats and move alongside them, touching their warmth, feeling the strength of their life. They're upset. They snatch at the grain, their hunger competing with Will's absence. I head into the bush, follow the track to where the horses camp and there he is, dropped, stiff. There's no struggle around him, no churned-up earth to say he fought death.

I stroke his nose. Everything around me hums. The tiny wrens in the gorse; the puzzled snuffling of the young mare smelling death; my labrador, sombre by my side.

So much is held in this old horse.

Home is not about a space, a garden, a house; it is not made by forcing something into being. It's about memory and the web of connections that stretch beyond the boundaries of our skin through the animals we live with. This old horse changed my small family. I'm different because he was in my life. For A, he was an anchor. He forced her to connect to something real, something outside her imagination. Later, C rode him too and his small-boy face alight with laughter at the antics of Will has stayed with me. For all of us this horse was a beginning.

I walk back to the house but I don't want to tell anyone he is gone, the same way I didn't want to tell them I thought he would die. I ring and cancel the vet's visit. She is comforting. I do tell J and he is all kindness. He hugs me and contacts a local contractor to ask him to come up and dig a hole to bury Will.

I ring A and tell her. She is upset but also practical. She is as far from that ethereal eight-year-old as I could have ever hoped. She is absolute in her certainty that I did the right thing in not bringing him into the stable or taking him down to Hobart. She said what a good death he had for an old horse. If he was thirteen when we bought him, which we highly doubt, he would now be twenty-nine. A fine life.

The paddock where Will is buried is now called Will's Flat and every time I cross it I give thanks for a horse that gave us a story to stand in while our trauma-shattered souls healed.

We fed out today. It took all afternoon and involved three vehicles with only two drivers and negotiating a stretch of highway thick with tourists. J and I are tired, our nerves ragged as the weeks drag on and it doesn't rain, doesn't look like it will rain, and there's no end in sight of the worst lambing season we've ever had. I find myself weeping in frustration when the sheep won't do what I want, or I lose my temper and scream so loudly I scratch my throat, but the sound is just plucked up by the wind so I know neither the tears nor the tantrum changes anything.

The drought is everywhere. It colours every thought, but because it is all-consuming we have learnt to be blind to the ways it places pressures on our relationship, on our friendships, on our extended family. We've learnt not to talk of it lest it sound trite, as if a rain would fix everything. I find my face takes on a frozen sort of grimace when people ask if we've had any rain, or, worse, say they saw on the national weather map that we'd had some rain. I also know I should be able to explain what a drought is and how it functions. But I realise if I articulate the fear, the psychological burden of being responsible for hungry animals, the heaviness of living under the daily pressure of having no water, of looking out on dying trees, of being part of a partnership that is failing on every level – if I start to say all that, where will it get me?

I should be getting dinner but I've snuck in here to sit for a moment and let the day shift through me. If I don't write it down, I think I will disappear. My computer screen sits on a copy of my PhD thesis. To write it I read hundreds of unpublished memoirs written by women on the frontiers of Australia and Canada in the nineteenth century. The sameness of their recordings made for boring reading at times but I suspected they wrote to make a trace and I disciplined myself to read into the repetitions, not to skip over them. But it's not until I am living this repetitive life that I understand. I was twenty-five when I was reading those women's lives. I thought they were writing to leave something permanent behind. But now I think they wrote so they could see themselves, so they did not disappear.

Today we drove past a rocky outcrop and both of us turned, remembering the time last year we found a ewe cast. She was startled into one more attempt to stand up, and struggled to her feet, only to crash to the ground again. I'd jumped out of the ute when it looked like she was going to run and when she fell I knelt on her as J followed slowly in the ute. I even grinned, I think, said, 'Your turn to find the lamb.' Then I caught sight of it. J had turned away, hadn't said anything. Some silence in him made me look again – it was dying, couldn't breathe though it sucked for air. J stood, stricken, said, 'I didn't see it.' He'd run it over. I realised this as we both stood and watched it die. The helplessness, the sheer wretched uselessness is etched into both of us. I turn and stand up the ewe.

So why write it down? Why not let the outcrop of rocks and tussocks hold that lamb's body and its quickly spilt life? Why write the trauma?

I don't think my grandmother would have wanted to know this story. I don't think my grandfather would have brought such stories to her. I think of her so often. She was from a different time, where it was harder to step out beyond the garden gate. Her energy, her considerable creativity were poured into her sewing; into a home layered with her art. She was intricately involved in the community, but she didn't involve herself in the farming. Sure, she would warm lambs back to life in her oven, make lunch for the stock agent and the bank manager, but as for running down a ewe or lying in the dirt, elbow-deep in birthing a lamb, no.

There's a part of me that would love to stand at the back door and wave J off, to turn inwards and apply myself only to the work of writing, but I can't. I can't because our world has shifted from one where collectively, as a society, we understood that life is fickle. I don't think we know this in the same way. We used to know, collectively, that death comes. Some of us still do, but it's not a shared knowledge; it's a quiet, sometimes shameful understanding in only those who have had death thrust on them.

So that's why I keep remembering, why I keep seeing the ones falling off the edge, why I need to keep witnessing the pain.

White-bellied sea eagle, *Halieetus leucogaster*, 70–90 cm,
span 2 metres.
Female larger.
Huge white and grey eagle. Cream legs and feet,
unfeathered.
Soars in majesty:
wings bold and upswept.
Short white tail,
dark near body,
gives it the look of a huge butterfly.
From underneath you may see
white and blackish triangles.
Cruel hook of beak, tear of talon.
Nest: altar of sticks, piled high in a living tree. Or, if on an island,
on the ground. Or, a remote coastal cliff.
Voice: far-carrying metallic clanking; mated pairs duet.
Hovers over prey, or makes sloping power-dive from a height (or
high perch) to seize from surface fish, waterbird or offal. Unlike
the osprey, seldom enters water.

Two metres. Pace it out. One large stride and then another. Then turn back and see the space. Then look up as a shadow passes and blocks the sun. Bet you did not think, *ahh, a butterfly*.

If I see you when I'm running on the beach I will stop, tilt my head, shade my eyes from the glare of sun on water and stand until my heart-thump recedes and my skin is pricked with cold.

I HAVEN'T BEEN TO THE BEACH these winter school holidays. I've told myself it is good to walk the dogs through the paddocks, good to be another set of eyes checking waterholes and unblocking feeders, but the real reason I haven't been back is that last time I went, I found something there that called up a rage so irrational it left me shaken.

I've grown addicted to the kick of cold, to plunging into water so clean and pure, so alive that it gives something elemental, something I don't realise I've lost until I find it again. The drought has made the beach even more worth my effort to get there. Though it's only ten minutes up the road, it is a world away from the farm. I drive out the gate and turn my back on hungry animals, whose heads all lift at the sound of a vehicle, and on domestic chores and tensions. The beach is new every time I walk over the sandhill. Sometimes the wind is blowing and the sand stings my face and I say to myself, 'You don't have to swim today, just get to the end.' But I always swim. Other times it's so cold it hurts my feet to run. Those times the water, which hovers around 12 to 13 degrees, is warmer than the air. Usually in winter I have the place to myself.

The day I lost my temper was as most others. There were no footprints ahead, just smooth, hard sand, the only patterns on it pricked by the feet of shore birds. The sea was almost still and whispered through its necklace of shells. The headland kept receding (as it does), but even as I put one foot in front of the other, ahead I could see, on the jutting rock shelf, an unfamiliar shape. I kept running and when I drew closer I saw it was a tower of rocks, with each rock carefully placed one on top of the other. A skyscraper. A phalanx. A statement. (J is always telling me I am prone to exaggeration.) I was shocked. I stopped running and stared. A stone stack. Someone had made a stone stack.

I'd read an article about the growing fad. Apparently, this is a social media phenomenon, a meditative process: people go to beautiful places and instead of simply sitting or swimming or walking around and looking at things, they gather rocks, stack them up and take a photograph to post on Instagram.

Now, there have been plenty of times when I have been walking in isolated and wonderful places and have felt myself on the edge of lost, have been walking with the uncomfortable feeling for a while, have wondered if I should turn back, have wondered if the faint hint of track was indeed a track or was in fact a wallaby pad, only to come across a little cairn of rocks, a sign reaching out from other walkers who have gone before who have felt the same almost-lost feeling and popped down a little pile of rocks to let those who come after know that they are on the right path.

This stack was not that.

I am not usually easily enraged. I hate destruction. I have never so much as carved my name in a desk, let alone been so sacrilegious as to mark a tree. I know other people come to this place. It pleases me that this beach is here for us all to wander along, each in our own world. And as for this tower of stone, I can see it's not hurting anyone. The headland is not a fragile ecosystem that is going to be disturbed by someone stacking rocks on top of each other. It's a rock shelf. The ocean moves rocks around on it effortlessly all the time. So mine is not the indignation of an ecowarrior. And yet I am furious. I clamber onto the platform, my bare feet wincing on the cold sharp stones. The tower is so tall it's almost head high. I lift the top stone and hurl it as far as I can into the sea. Then I push hard and the whole structure topples onto the platform. I'm surprised at how much strength it takes to knock over the tower, and when it finally falls it smashes, rock on rock, and I'm filled with adrenalin and a sudden kind of pathetic remorse. And then I don't care. I strip and run into the water, swim, stay in longer than normal, catch a little wave, and another, and then come out, dress quickly and run back up the beach. I get in the car, drive up the dirt road and am home.

But my act of destruction has stayed with me. It's kept me from the beach all through the school holidays and I've missed the benediction of salt.

Then one morning as I sit at my desk and watch the sky streak orange, mauve and finally firefly-pink, I need to go to the beach.

When the dogs see me heading for the ute rather than off on our usual walk, they are delirious with joy. They love the ride, are giddy with anticipation, and no matter my mood, they infect me. We arrive and the dashboard says it's 4 degrees. Balmy. The beach is there, waiting for us.

The tower is back. Not quite so tall, though I suspect it has taken a battering from the breaking waves. I strip and dive in, feel myself shrink and for a moment am slapped back by the cold. I've learnt that if I don't fight it, if I still myself, accept it, it creeps away and I feel myself expand again, just a little, enough to take a breath. I dive beneath a wave and my skull tightens. The winter swells are here and though it's not big from the shore, once I get out in it I feel the fierceness of the undertow, the isolation, and I duck beneath the surface, find the sand beneath my feet, push into my stroke and catch a swell back to the beach. The dogs dance with delight in the shallows and I walk back to my pile of clothes. The air, which I had tried to shield myself from before my swim, is now friendly. I dress and climb on to the platform to look at the tower. Then, as deliberately and carefully as the person who had constructed it, I take each stone, and place it gently among its brethren. I work with the peace I have when I sit in front of the fire and embroider, or when I weed the garden. Over and over I place the rocks back on the platform until the small ledge where the tower was is empty.

My brother rings when I'm on my way home. I tell him about my morning. He's fascinated by my earlier fury. He understands the frustration at the social media performance of it, the need to be seen, but, he asks, what if it's more than that? And I say, of course it's more than that. It's the claiming of a place that is not ours to claim. The place just is. You have to come ready to accept whatever it has to give you. It waits for any of us, every one of us can receive what it has to give. It is washed over and over, worn away. Massive boulders shifted, sand moved from one end of the beach to the other. Eventually the sea, the wind, the tide would have taken care of the tower of stones, but, I say, I couldn't wait for the slow collapse.

My brother laughs. He's amused by the story – our parallel lives, both of us walking our dogs, wanting something more; my reaction at having my world tilted a little. I see how absurd it might seem. I tell him that whoever built the tower is welcome to build it again. But I will again – with respect – take it down.

spring

Graft (noun)

1. A shoot or scion inserted into a slit made in another plant or stock, from which the shoot receives sap and on which it grows.
2. The place in stock where a scion is inserted.
3. The process of grafting; an instance of grafting.
4. A piece of living tissue surgically transplanted to another place on the same organism, or to another organism, so that it might grow; the process of transplanting tissue for this purpose.

GRAFT (NOUN, COLLOQUIAL)

1. Work, especially hard work.

GRAFT (NOUN, COLLOQUIAL)

1. Illicit gain, especially in connection with politics or business; the practices used to secure this, especially bribery, blackmail, or the abuse of one's power or influence.

GRAFT (VERB)

1. a) Insert or fix in or on so as to produce a vital or indissoluble union.

b) Join together (two unfinished or broken pieces of knitting) by weaving an extra row of stitches between the pieces.

2. Fix graft or grafts on (a stock). Also, produce (fruit) by grafting.
3. Transplant (a piece of living tissue) surgically to another place on the same organism, or to another organism.

The Shorter Oxford English Dictionary doesn't include sheep in its examples of the word 'graft', but that's what I do. Grafting: the act of joining together two things to make them one – a motherless lamb to a lambless mother.

Mud Map

A mud map is drawn in the dirt, with a stick or a finger. It's the sketchiest and most ephemeral of maps. A map that cannot be consulted again, but must be remembered.

GOLDEN WHISTLER, *Pachycephala pectoralis*, 16.5–18.5 cm.
Male: head/breast-band black, separating white throat
from rich gold-yellow nape-band
and underparts; grey with
black tip.
Female: grey-brown above, progressively washed deeper olive-green
from south-east Australia to Queensland;
pale tups to wing-coverts
(from subtle sing) or double line across wing.
Underparts grey-buff.

Bill black, stubby (Tasmania) to longish (Queensland).
Pairs when
breeding,
otherwise solitary, or in mixed-species companies.
In spring,
both sexes display, duet,
sing vivaciously,
with see-saw posturing.
Voice: many sweet notes;
brisk *sweetawit, sweetawit*
rising *Wheet-wheat-wheat-WHITTLE!* (like a whip crack)
brisk *dee-dee-dee-ah-WHIT*

Breeds: August to January.
Nest: rough cup of bark strips,
spider web, stems, rootlets,
skeleton leaves, fern fronds, grass, twigs.

You will need to look low in blackberries, tree ferns, long grass or an upright fork (1–4 m high).

Eggs: 2–3; oval; white/cream/salmon-pink; freckled, dotted, blotched, red-brown, grey, dark brown, black; underlying spots of lavender/dark grey.

I watched a golden whistler hawk a moth from the sky.

The insect was almost as big as the whistler, that snappiest of dressers, and the little bird flew to a sapling, where he beat the moth against a branch.

I stood, face turned up, as he tried to swallow the fluttering, whirring furred creature. Did I laugh? Perhaps.

The bird flew off, still weighted with ambition, and I was left alone to brush the falling moth dust from my eyes.

Up the hill I walked, through the layers of termites and ants, past centipedes and through spider webs, up and up alongside frogs, in clouds of mosquitoes, past potoroos and wallabies, past wombats and a snuffling echidna, a blind woman, save for the soft coating of moth fur on my skin.

SPRING HERE STARTS SLOWLY. The first hint is in the stretch of the days: the light comes earlier and stays later. Harder to notice is the warming earth, with blasts of bright sun in between the sleet and threatening snow. Into this tumble the lambing starts.

Our ewes have been scanned (pregnancy-tested) in winter when their lambs are still secrets. They are separated into those having multiples, singles; or dry ewes. The multiples, or 'twinners', are put on the best pasture we have, which this year is just one more variation on bone-dry. As the days lengthen we bring them back into the yards and give them a long-acting pre-lambing drench. We walk them slowly back to their lambing paddocks, and we wait.

We join our ewes later in the autumn so they lamb further into spring in the hope of gentler weather and better pasture.

When lambing starts I give myself over to a different rhythm. Every year the time of lambing passes in a blur of early mornings, long days and broken nights, and I find it hard to tease out what exactly fills my days. This year there is nothing in the paddocks for the ewes to eat. They will survive on pellets and hay, but they will have to walk to find good water that is neither brackish nor heavy with mud. Instinct will battle with the genetics of the ewe. She has been bred because her mother was a good mother. But there is an older knowledge passed down – that to live, a ewe must walk away from her lamb. Only the ewes with the strongest mothering instinct will raise a lamb this year, and because of it they themselves might grow so weak they'll die.

A newborn lamb should meet the world front hooves first. After the tips of its hooves, the tip of a nose comes next, and then, when the ewe's contractions bear down, a head with ears flattened. All going well, the ewe will pause and catch her breath, pant for a moment and then push again, and the lamb's shoulders will emerge. Now the ewe might stand and the lamb will spill from her, slippery with the sluice of birth. When things work as they should, the ewe will turn and begin to lick and chew that lamb, working her rough tongue across its ribs, tickling its lungs. When things work as they should, the lamb will shake its head, splutter the birth from its nose and open its mouth. It will take its first breath. The breath will not be quite a breath, but a bubble of a breath, a suggestion, not tender but ragged and desperate. It will take another and another and with each it will grow more alive. Its ears, pinned to its head by the passage of its birth, will loosen and it will peer at the world through milky eyes. Heat from the inside of its mother's body will meet the cold world and steam will shroud it. In minutes the just-born lamb will stand. Its four soft hooves will harden and set while its mother licks and licks, her tongue colouring in its shape. Across the earth it will stagger, seeking more of life, the hot swelling of its mother's udder. Often the ewe will spin and lick and spin and lick, but gradually she will quieten and the lamb will find her udder and taste the thickly sweet colostrum.

When things work as they should, this happens over and over in corners of paddocks, beneath gums and gorse, out in the open or in the sheltered overhang of a creek bank. And the miracle is that though I detail the ragged edges of this – the deaths, the near-misses, the hard-won victories – for the most part the majority of our ewes lamb quickly, without intervention or witness. But in a season such as this, when the rain hasn't come, when the creeks are empty and the dams shrunken to a putrid mess of muddied slime – in this season it is only the strong who will survive.

Why, then, do I insist on inserting myself? Why can't I let the weak die and nature take its relentless course?

In her book *When Women Were Birds*, the American writer Terry Tempest Williams describes lying with her mother as she drew near to death. Williams says her mother was 'dying in the same ways she was living, consciously'. Williams was thirty-one, her mother was fifty-four. She remembers curling her body around her mother as they lay under the weightless warmth of a mohair rug. Williams rubbed her mother's back, feeling the vertebrae through her mother's skin like rungs of a ladder. Her mother said, 'I am leaving you my journals, but you must promise me that you will not look at them until after I am gone.' Williams gave her word. She had not known her mother kept journals.

Her mother died a week later, in the dead of winter on a night when the moon was encircled by ice crystals. Williams waited a cycle of the moon, until her family home was empty. There were three shelves of beautiful clothbound books. The books were perfectly aligned, spine against the lip of the shelves. She reached for the first and opened it. It was empty. So were the second and third. Shelf after shelf of empty journals.

As a fifty-four-year-old woman, the same age her mother was when she died, Williams wrote of her younger self, 'The blow of her blank journals became a second death.'

'My mother's journals are paper tombstones,' she wrote. 'I didn't realise how young she was, but isn't that the conceit of mothers – that we conceal our youth and exist only for our children? It is the province of mothers to preserve the myth that we are unburdened without our own problems … When women were birds, we knew otherwise. We knew our greatest freedom was in taking flight at night, when we could steal the heavenly darkness for ourselves, navigating through the intelligence of stars and the constellations of our own making in the delight and terror of our uncertainty. What my mother wanted to do and what she was able to do remains her secret.'

My mother wrote in a journal. Every morning. In her own hieroglyphics. I have never tried to crack her code. Like Williams, I need to let my mother's silences remain. In this season of want I'm shifting through my memory to find a deeper knowledge, something my mother gifted me that I have not yet understood.

Words that are useful to know

MATRESCENCE

Coined in 1973 by the medical anthropologist Dana Raphael, matrescence means 'to become a mother'. In 2017 psychiatrist Alexandra Sacks wrote an article in the *New York Times*, 'The Birth of a Mother', which referenced matrescence, and when her piece went viral the term jumped back into the vocabulary of motherhood. Now, fifty years after Raphael first used the word, the science of this event in a woman's life is a burgeoning field. And any woman who has become a mother knows it is, as Sacks puts it, 'one of the most significant physical and psychological changes a woman will ever experience'. Like puberty and menopause, it's shape-shifting.

IT'S OUR LAST FEED RUN BEFORE LAMBING STARTS. We creep up the lane past mobs of pregnant ewes and drop over the crest of the hill with flats spreading out on both sides. J is in the tractor; a bag filled with a tonne of sheep pellets sways from the forks. C and I are in utes. I have 2 tonnes of pellets on the back, C's ancient ute (his fourteenth birthday present bought from a bloke in the pub for four hundred bucks) strains with its load. We hope this run will last the ewes until the majority of them have lambed.

On either side of the lane the flats are divided into different paddocks by wire fences and stands of ancient poplars bare against a brilliant blue sky. When I am out walking I often feel the pressing need to lie on the earth and stare up at them. I can feel them stretching: their roots web through the chocolate soil to the invisible river flowing deep beneath; above me their trunks are like ship masts or a witch's broomstick. Today, ewes graze beneath their bare tips and our convoy of vehicles crawls past, hoping to be no more than a ripple on the surface. My hands are tight on the steering wheel. I slowly creep past a mob of older Merino ewes scanned in lamb with singles. We mix fifty or so of these older ewes in with the maidens – the quaint name for young ewes who have never had a lamb.

In the distance, I can see a maiden ewe has lambed. The main mob has wandered away from her and she's stressed. Behind her, a tiny white blob staggers to its feet. The ewe is maybe fifteen metres from it, walking towards the rest of her mob, whose attention is turned by our slow passage up the lane. This is one of the breed characteristics we select – that the ewe will stay with her lamb, not abandon it when we get close – but this is no ordinary year, the first-time mother is tense with hunger, and the tractor means food. The lamb calls and calls. I wonder at the brutality of nature. Say the instinct of the lamb to call wasn't strong, then it would probably live only a few hours. Instead, I watch as it bends into its bleating, its whole body arched in longing. Across the bare ground its young mother flicks her ear, stops and turns back. The lamb staggers towards her and when it reaches her she bends over and starts to lick it. Her hormones will surge as she licks, they will drown out the noise of our convoy.

She has become a mother.

Further up the lane I pass a single tiny lamb curled in a tight ball on the dam wall. Over the two-way radio J's voice breaks in. 'Did you see that?'

'Yep,' I say.

'Yeah,' he says. 'It was there this morning.'

I don't press the talk button for a moment. A part of me doesn't want to know, wants to drive past, wants to tell myself a story of how its mother planted it there and would be back to get it.

'I'll check it on the way back,' I say. I know it will still be there.

Our vehicles pass through a paddock of bush, then down a steep creek bank and across its dry stony bed. J has the gate swung wide by the time I get there and he is back on the tractor. The wind is fierce and whips dust off the paddock as we fill the lick feeders. Each feeder holds 2 tonnes of pellets. We've bought two feeders for each mob of ewes. It's an experiment born of desperation: J has been feeding for months by dragging a fertiliser spreader behind the tractor, which dispenses the pellets over the paddock. This has worked well. It stops the greedy feeders from pushing the shy feeders off the trail of pellets and slows hungry sheep from gorging themselves. But he can't feed like this in lambing. The sheep stampede the tractor and in the chaos newborn and young lambs are abandoned. So the lick feeders are a compromise. We hope they nourish the ewes while minimising mismothering.

The mob bunches at a safe distance as the pellets spill into the feeders. The sheep can smell them and circle us restlessly. Off on her own at the edge of some timber a ewe stands over her new lamb, which doesn't move. I pull myself onto the back of the ute and look at the pair through the binoculars. The lamb looks dead. Its mother ignores our presence, the smell of the pellets, the restless mob, the stirring dust, the raw wind. She nudges the still body.

When the feeders are full we make our way home. I stay back and close the gates behind us. Driving up the lane I see the lamb is still curled on the western wall of the dam. I stop the ute and turn off the engine. A scarlet robin flicks from the ground to perch on the wire fence. His breast is a fierce, bright red. He flits his way up the wire. I get out, wish him well and slide through the fence. The lamb is curled on the baked earth of the dam wall. Instinct has told it to flatten its body against the warm earth out of the wind. I make a *baaing* noise. It makes no call in reply and is too weak to run away from me; even when I pick it up it just hangs in my hand. The fight is out of it. It's floppy. Abandoned. I put it in the cabin of the ute and drive home.

Dust (noun)

1. Finely powdered earth, other matter lying on the ground or on surfaces or carried about by the wind.
   Any substance pulverised; fine particles of matter.
2. (The material of) the human frame.
   A dead person's remains.
   As the type of that which is worthless or contemptible, or occupies the lowest position.
3. A particle of something: a pinch of something.
4. A cloud of finely powdered earth or other fine particles floating in the air.

   Confusion, turmoil, disturbance.

   Slang: A row, an uproar
5. Money, cash.
6. An *act* of cleaning by wiping off dust.

Bite the dust. Bull-dust. Cosmic dust. Dry as dust. Dust and ashes. Happy dust. In the dust (dead and buried). Kiss the dust (to fall with force). Not see someone for dust (to leave with haste). Shake the dust off my feet (depart indignantly or disdainfully). Throw dust in a person's eye (mislead, distract). Wait until the dust settles (calm the fuck down). Dust bowl (land made unproductive by wind erosion of soil, especially following loss of vegetation through drought or rapacious farming practices). Dust bath (to roll in dust to clean feathers or fur). Dust-box (a box from which a fine powder is sprinkled to dry ink). Dust bunny (a ball of dust and fluff, poor man's velvet). Dust devil (a moving whirlwind of dust, a dust storm, a whirly whirly). Dust disease (pneumoconiosis, black lung, miner's lung). Dust up (fight). Dustless (*a moment*).

WHEN MY SON WAS SMALL, four years old or thereabouts, he did not speak very much. Perhaps I should have been worried. My older brother has never spoken. But C's silence seemed part of his personality, he *could* speak and chose not to, so I let him be. It was a time when absence was heavy around me and the hours of the day long. It was a time, like now, of drought, and the dirt where we lived was loosened by the hooves of sheep and cattle. Each long afternoon I would take the children to the stables and saddle Will and, as the sun sank, my daughter would ride. She would make patterns in the dust, tracing figures of eight and clover leaf etchings on the bare earth, and with each performance a fear was quietened and something in the steadiness of the horse rose up and strengthened her. While she rode, my son would push his toy dump truck loaded with pebbles, twigs and dirt. When he grew tired of making roads

I would take a stick and draw sums in the dust. 4 + 5 = …, 10 + 12 = … and so on and so forth. He would follow me and write the answers. Over the days of the drought the sums would grow more complex until he was able to carry numbers backwards and forwards. He would start school the next year and the drought would have broken.

When he first went to school, the sagging relief of time to myself saw me waste (did I?) almost his entire kindergarten year. I wandered through those days heady with indecision about what I should be doing. My task of editing a non-fiction book seemed too big for the hours between nine and three, and yet his schooling seemed limitless, as did the sentence of my motherhood. And it did feel like a sentence, a sentence I had stepped into willingly, only to have the shock of my husband's illness and death mean motherhood became something different, a deeper and more profound responsibility and also something that came to define me in a way I had not ever been defined before.

Now, in the grip of another drought, the end of C's schooling is almost here. I can count the number of school holidays we have left. What was once a cycle without end is no longer. It makes these last few school holidays feel weighted.

Realistically, what these holidays will hold for C and me is work. This time next year he will be on the cusp of independence. This time next year I will be actively encouraging him to leave home. I will be helping him find his way forward, away from me. I feel it already, like another loss. I have the strongest sensation of the duality of time rushing ever faster and deeper beneath my feet while I walk above, quiet and slow, the days marked by the ordinary. Every so often the river rises, and I see how fast it's flowing, and I'm stunned.

I get out to open the gate and see a mess of plucked wool and a black cloak of crows. J signals he'll check the ewe. If she's still alive he'll slit her throat to end her suffering. I try to imagine myself as a lamb, prey only to the most base instincts, pushed by wind to shelter, hunted away from maternal safety by a chorus of murderers. J tosses the body of the ewe onto the tray of the ute.

I crouch. Make my voice low and baaaa, *long and desperate. From the bracken, under a fallen branch of gum, hidden from a crow's beak or eagle's talon, is her lamb. He's safe from predators but so close to death. His birth coat is still on him, a second skin, now, hours after his birth, hard like eggshell. His mother has birthed him and was then too weak to stand; she was attacked, but her lamb fought to breathe, fought to stand and then sought shelter. I pull it out of the bracken and grunt, because what is there to say.*

In the maidens there's a young ewe in all sorts of trouble. Her lamb is dead – one leg forward and one leg back, stuck fast, eyes and tongue are gone, eaten by crows. J eases the little creature from her. We put the ewe on the back of the ute. If she doesn't die I'll foster the lamb at my feet on to her.

All this before 8 am.

Back home and I have a fight to save the lamb. I milk the ewe's colostrum into its mouth, drip by precious drip. It sucks reluctantly. I check on it at dusk. It's floppy and unresponsive. Only hours ago it had been up and interested in its foster mother. I take it back to the house and when J sees it, for the second time offers to knock it on the head. Nope, I say, and mix a dose of colostrum up. The lamb lies in front of the fire, almost lifeless. The dogs sniff it and arrange themselves as near the heat as possible. The house stinks of lamb. Of death and almost life. I drip the warm colostrum down its throat. J looks at me like I'm mad to keep this up, and most probably I am.

I wrap it up and put it under the wood heater.

Two hours later it's shaking its head. When I pick it up and put the rubber teat in its mouth it sucks down more colostrum. Four hours later and it's up on its four legs demanding milk. The young ewe in the yards will mother it tomorrow, but for tonight she can pull at the grass in the yards, eat the sheep nuts I've placed near her, drink the fresh clean water and lick at the hay and mend. The lamb, its belly full, can spend the night by the fire.

Grey butcherbird, *Cracticus torquatus*, 24–30 cm.
Other names: silver-backed butcherbird,
Derwent or Tasmanian jackass.
Voice: loud, musical,
piping duet.
Aggressive
predator.
Perches and pounces.
Beak strong, hooked.
Impales prey, including nestlings, often to be eaten later.

I was a curious six-year-old when I asked my grandfather to tell me about the butcherbird. Why that name?

My grandfather didn't answer, just stood and mimicked the pure, mellow notes that dropped like pearls from the throat of the black-and-white-suited fellow *Cracticus nigrogularis*, the pied butcherbird, who patrolled the edge of the garden. Bob, as we called my grandfather, pointed with his walking stick. 'Look at his beak.'

The bird's beak was a vicious hook.

Bob was cutting up meat for his dogs on an old stump outside the back door. I was sitting on the back step and asking questions. I asked too many questions. Of everyone. The shrug of adult annoyance seemed to precede me. The bird flapped lazily from the gate to the guttering waiting for my grandfather to toss him a piece of meat.

My grandfather said, 'He's a vicious one, eats little birds for breakfast.'

'Is he called a butcherbird because he watches the butcher's block?'

Often my grandfather would not answer my first question. Instead he'd let them pile up. Under his hands the hunk of meat divided into four. *Thwack* went the cleaver. His black labrador snuffled at the edges of the stump looking for chips of bone flung from the cleaver's blade. The bird cocked its head. My grandfather took a strip of fat edged with red flesh and tossed it into the air. The bird swooped and plucked it from the sky.

'Watch him,' he said, and went to feed his dogs.

I followed the bird to the line of poplar trees along the

garden fence. There he landed and instead of gulping down his morsel as I expected, he poked the strip of meat in the fork of a poplar branch and using his beak he stripped the meat from the fat. My grandfather walked over, his gait uneven, his heavy boots crunching the crisp fallen leaves. We both looked up at the bare branch.

'Do you see now?'

I didn't really, so I said nothing.

'He's called a butcherbird because he hangs his meat up like a butcher. Listen for him tonight just as the sun goes down.'

Here, there are no pied butcherbirds. The notes in my bird book all date my sightings on the mainland. I miss the way their song drips through the evening air, each note distilled. 'Superb slow, flute-like, mellow notes,' George Adams says in *The Complete Guide to Australian Birds*, and I think, well exactly. We have the grey butcherbird, and if you hadn't heard the pied butcherbird you would think the grey has a melodic song. But his voice doesn't trip and drip as if he is playing with sound. The Tasmanian butcherbird is smaller, plainer. It has taken me a while to forgive him these things.

Then again, grey is a misnomer. His head and face are black, his back grey and neck graced with a thin white collar. His wings are grey but if you watch closely you will see, as he flies overhead, that he is white beneath. You'll be able to tell if the bird is a male or a female as the 'she' butcherbird is larger and browner. They build their nests high, ten metres or so in a whippy sapling or in a scrubby tree, a mess of twigs lined with grass. Their eggs can be dull green, or grey-brown, or pale grey, or spotted and flecked with brown as if paint has been dripped carelessly from a fine brush. It falls to the female to sit on the eggs, but once the eggs hatch, the whole family raises them – even the teenagers stick around to help.

There is a family of grey butcherbirds that lives between the cottage and the creek. Their territory includes a stand of tall blackwoods that dip their toes in the creek; beyond these are eucalypts whose roots cling to the rocky, clay-clogged slope beneath the cottage. The butcherbirds watch me as I go about my work. They also watch the superb blue wrens, the grey fantail, the spotted pardalotes, the robins, the thornbills, the silver eyes – all the little birds that over-winter here. The world around me is layered in beauty and death and we are part of it.

EARLY THIS MORNING THE SUN WAS WARM, the day felt benign and gentle. Now the wind has sprung up and I'm wishing I'd worn my thick sheepskin jacket. J checks the sheep feeders and I walk across the bare paddock to the beehives set along the edge of the dry creek bank. They are owned by our local beekeeper and in exchange for a tub of honey, he brings his bees to spend the winter here. But now the only thing for them is the gorse and he must come to supplement their feed with sugar-sweetened water. They're busy, though, a swirl of them in and out of their hives.

I get back in the ute, we push on, cross the creek and I open the next gate. This gate is usually a good one – well swung and with plenty of chain – but the drought changes everything. The earth shrinks from around the fence posts, so they list in the prevailing winds. Now the chain is tight and I have to wrestle with it each morning. My hands are sore. They ache every night when I get into bed. Tapping the keyboard, holding a pen, these things do not build the strength needed to wrestle reluctant ewes all day. My fingers are tender and swollen with the tiny broken tips of gorse ends hidden in the wool. I finally unlatch the gate and when I get back to the ute J points to a big crossbred ewe standing over a dead lamb. We know her – J even has a name for her, he calls her Doris. She has a dicky back leg and walks with a distinctive gait, which is not unlike J's, with his arthritic hip and knee. It's a mystery how she even gets pregnant, but she always raises a good lamb. She's getting older, though, and I meant to take her out of the mob when we scanned the ewes so she could have her lamb where I could keep an eye on her.

Her head is up as we drive past. J says he reckons I could run her down and use her to raise an abandoned lamb we picked up yesterday. I shake my head – I'm not up to the task today. I'm thinking we should just let her mourn her lamb and get on with the business of survival in this awful season. 'Look at the milk on her,' J says. I'm feeling tired and pathetic. 'Let's see what else we find,' I mutter.

We drive through the timber and do a lap of the paddock, but as we head towards the next gate we see Doris off by herself. 'It's meant to be,' says J and grins at me. Next thing, we are flying across the paddock in the ute. Doris is like a refrigerator on legs and when she starts to tire J yells at me to go and I leap out of the door and sprint. I block her in the corner of the paddock, she turns and faces me, but this is no lightweight Merino ewe – she props to the right and left and then she looks me in the eye and charges straight through me. I grab at her as she knocks me down – it's like trying to stop a log truck. I lie on the dirt, bruised and winded. But J doesn't give up – he manages to grab her with his shepherd's crook. Between the two of us we get her onto the ute. J puts a chain around her neck and both front legs. She glares at us. Usually when we put the Merino ewes on their backs they stay there, docile and accepting of their fate. Not so Doris. Every ounce of her wants to break free. I tell her I've got a lamb for her. I'm not sure this is something she wants.

In the next paddock we see a ewe with a lamb's swollen head sticking out of her. The stuck lamb looks dead, but if we don't deliver it, the ewe will die a horrible death. Of course, the ewe with the stuck lamb is right next to a ewe who has just lambed – her newborn is up on shaky legs; it must be only fifteen minutes old. We back off and approach from a different paddock. I climb through the fence and work my way between the two ewes. The ewe with the stuck lamb I catch easily. The other ewe doesn't move from her lamb and I whisper my thanks as I ease the stricken ewe onto her side and grab the protruding leg of the dead lamb. It's really stuck, no way was she getting this one out. When I pull harder she groans. I swear this is worse when you've had children. I murmur my sympathy and keep a steady tension on the lamb's leg until I feel the release of its shoulder. Then I can grab both legs and pull. The lamb comes in a rush. I drag the ewe to the fence. J pulls her through and the two of us swing her onto the ute to take back to the yards where she can be a foster mother.

The last paddock we check has been problem-free. Until today. Right on the edge of the bush, through the binoculars J spots a ewe, legs kicking, but well cast. We drive in, creep round the mob, which takes no notice of us. The ewe has dug herself into the ground, her afterbirth trailing behind her. There is no sign of her lamb. We find it finally, fifty metres away, deep in the bush. At least it survived.

Back at the yards we unload three ewes and one lamb. The ewe who has been cast is having trouble standing. The lamb wants nothing to do with her; that crucial moment to mother them up is gone. It will now take patience to establish. We're both tired and J loses his temper at the lamb who refuses its mother and the ewe who refuses her lamb, so we leave them all and go home for a cuppa.

The house is full of washing and jobs. I hang clothes out. Clean up breakfast. Finally, I make a coffee and sit on the couch for a moment. This is a mistake: fatigue is a swamp I can't give in to because although the housework can wait, the lamb I want to foster on to Doris will not.

C, home on school holidays, comes over to the yards to help me. He is all energy and fluid movement: where I climb over the fences, he puts a hand on the top rail and vaults. I introduce Doris to the beautiful Merino lamb I've had on the bottle for two nights and she's so affronted by the whole thing she tries to kill it. I have to get into the race with her, pin her, and put the lamb on to her udder. It sucks like a good thing, and she slams forwards and back. I wrestle with her for twenty minutes while the lamb has a drink and then it's my turn to lose my temper properly – I yell so hard I hurt my voice and turn and kick the gate. The lamb won't suck, the ewe won't let her milk down. C looks on in amazement as I cry a little bit. He comes over and helps me; tips her over for me and holds her while I convince the lamb that it has to have a drink if it wants to live. It seems determined to die.

We get back to the house at 2.30 for lunch. I lie on the couch and fall asleep instantly until it's time to go out and fill feeders. At least this job means I don't have to wrestle sheep.

By the time we get back and the mothers in the yards are fed and I've wrestled with reluctant ewes to feed newly grafted lambs, I realise I haven't got dry sheets for the bed. And we have to go out tonight. Lambing in a drought is hell.

The lamb on Doris survives the night but it's having trouble getting its mouth around her engorged udder. I milk her a little and the lamb latches on and sucks hard while I hold its reluctant foster mother. If a sheep could growl that is what she would be doing. Our furies match each other. I wedge her between the side of the race with my body. She's pinned again. She feeds the lamb.

Overnight, the ewe and lamb that made both J and I lose our tempers have mothered up well. I move a few of the pairs I've been working with up out of their small individual yards and into a bigger yard. Here, I can still keep an eye on them, and it's the first step to them being absorbed back into the bigger population of the mob. I wonder if midwives feel this way as they send the mothers with babies they've delivered into the world. They cease to be individuals and become part of the system again. From this big yard the sheep move to another bigger yard, and from there out into one of the house paddocks, with its sheltering tree line.

C comes with us on the lambing run. His humour, his youth change the atmosphere in the ute cabin. In Dry Creek there's a ewe with a stuck lamb surrounded by other ewes, each with newborns. We need to catch her without mismothering the ewes with new lambs. We put some pressure on the small group; the mothers mutter nervously but they stay with their new lambs. The ewe with the stuck lamb sets off away from them. She runs with her hind legs splayed wide by the lamb half-birthed, stuck fast. I hate watching this. The lamb is still alive. Its head flops from side to side with each stride she takes. C is out the door of the ute and has her run down in about five metres. He's so much faster than me. She jigs to dodge him, and though he slips, he's still quick enough to counter her change in direction and has the lamb pulled by the time J and I get to them. I sit in the warm cabin as they load up the ewe and the just-delivered lamb onto the back. We are out of there in moments, leaving the other new mothers in peace.

There is another story of mothering.

I'm on the second day of a battle with a ewe with a green tag in her ear. The green tag indicates she is three years old. She also has a little nick in her ear, which tells me she was dry (scanned in lamb but didn't raise it) in her maiden year. This is her second year as a potential mother. Because the seasons have been so tough J has given those maidens who didn't raise a lamb last year one more chance, but two strikes and they will either run with wethers or be sold. Watching this one's behaviour over the last two days, I would bet she had a lamb last year and left it. She's a beautiful ewe, a real supermodel. Her wool is luminous, she has a noble head, well-set ears and her feet are perfect. She is exactly what we are breeding for – except she is not, because she wants nothing to do with her own lamb. Yesterday, while we were checking her mob from the hill, I watched her through the binoculars. I was a witness as she had her lamb and then walked off without even looking at it. There was no disturbance to make her do that. She hadn't seen the ute parked in the shelter of the trees on the hill. No other ewe was around to interfere. The mob was peaceful. We drove into the paddock and caught her before she could rejoin the mob. I walked over and picked up the lamb. It was wet with birth, a beautiful ram lamb. The ewe now has a black tag in her ear to say she will be culled from our breeding program, but before this happens I am determined she is going to raise this lamb. If I succeed, the lamb will become a wether and give us a beautiful fleece every year for the next six or seven. Its mother's bad mothering genes will not be passed on.

I've put them in a small yard and the lamb is an absolute battler. It keeps pestering its mother for a drink but she won't stand for it, butts it away, even; if I hadn't watched the lamb slip from her body I wouldn't believe it was hers. I catch her and hold her still. The lamb drinks.

This is a season of abandonment. The conditions are so hard that something deep in some of the ewes tells them to walk away from their lambs, to leave them to drift in front of the wind, to curl and quietly die. Last year was the same, so perhaps this ewe is saving her genetics for the right season to raise a lamb. Or perhaps she is simply not a mother.

Watching this, I'm confronted with my childhood. I am circling back, looking for the things I saw and have forgotten, or what I saw and didn't understand. I'm caught on the cusp of a version of motherhood my own mother never experienced. One of her children never left her. I try to imagine her life if she had walked away from my older brother. I cannot understand her without understanding what mothering a child so demanding, so otherworldly, so difficult would have done to her.

Poke eye, pull hair, throw glass, plate or vase, wet pants, flood sink, bath, block toilet, stamp feet, smack face, scratch face, bite arm, shit.

These were just some of the weapons my brother had at his disposal. Some of the ways he expressed his frustration, his rage, his impotence in the face of a world that would not accept his difference. To help him my mother would take him walking. They would walk early in the morning, then again before lunch, then again in the afternoon. The movement soothed something in my brother and it gave my mother a sort of break because she could mostly just follow him. There was always the fear that we would lose him, that my mother would glance away and he might be gone. This happened over and over again. He was here – still for a moment, the house relaxed, perhaps my mother was cooking, talking to a friend on the phone – and then he was gone.

His 'running away' was so familiar that it had no sting in it for my younger brother and me. We stopped fearing it. Perhaps too we wished him his freedom. Out walking, he would sing in his tuneless, wordless voice and the sound would break your heart because it was shameless joy. Besides, he always turned up, so I could never see what the panic was all about. Why not just enjoy a few drama-free hours? We would say, my younger brother and I, he loves it. He needs to walk, why not just let him be?

Not so my mother, who would call around the neighbourhood to ask people to watch for him and then get in the car to check all the places he might be.

My mother did abandon my brother – or so she thought. Every week she would drive him to a boarding school, a Steiner school in the Hills District of Sydney. It wasn't far from my school and on Monday mornings my mother would drive us both. She would drop me first and then my brother. What I didn't see was my mother weeping the whole way home.

She later told me of the pain of those trips and of course I had never thought of her or my brother driving onward. All I wanted was not to be seen getting out of the car in which sat a desperate-looking woman and my brother rocking in the front seat, biting his arm, banging his head, screeching his wordless goodbye.

Now I'm a mother I know she did this for my younger brother and me. We got to play at normalcy. Of course, by that stage it was too late.

My brother spent a decade at this place, staying there during the week and coming home on weekends, moving from the school section to the workshop. But he was never happy and as soon as she could my mother brought him home for good. Bad things, terrible things, had happened to him there. And as if his life was not hard enough he is blind in one eye from someone attacking him and scratching him so badly his left eye has a thick film of scar tissue across it. No one except my mother seemed outraged.

My son started boarding school in Year 6. He was eleven years old.

The first drive home after dropping him off felt like one of the longest of my life. And I was lucky – I'd left a laughing, excited, nervous but distracted small boy enthusiastically playing table tennis. He'd barely had time to say goodbye. I never had to deal with tears, or even much homesickness. Six years on and I can see my son is loved and respected. And yet I still have an ache, an unease, a pain under my ribs from the memory of those drives home, having left him in an institution that, no matter how homey, was not home.

Now, as he nears the end of his schooling, I know the rightness of the experience of boarding for him. Yet this knowledge is bittersweet. A thousand small moments not lived. Not kissing him goodnight every night, not being there for the first day of term, or his birthdays. Not being there to share in his small victories, or commiserate over the stings of lost football matches. They're all small things and I think more significant for me than him. He was surrounded by great mentors who gave him a glimpse of how he could move through a world that was bigger than our family unit. But for me sending a child to boarding school was the instinctive opposite to the conception I had of myself as a mother. So I had misgivings about doing it, but not regrets. I let this knowledge sit alongside my mothering loss.

My mother had no such comfort in sending her child away from her, yet she did it for my younger brother and me. But she was never free. The only way she would ever abandon my brother was in death. And she fought against that with every fibre of her being.

J sees me struggling with the now black-tagged ewe in the yards. 'You can't win 'em all,' he says. 'I know,' I reply, 'but I'm winning this one.'

Today we bring home three ewes, and spot a sea eagle circling and maybe fifty murdering crows. We see flashes of red and yellow and blue – parrots across a dusty paddock. I try to take in all I'm being asked to see. It's impossible. The life and death of it, heave, swell and sigh.

IN TASMANIA, SPRING MEANS FOOTBALL FINALS. Everyone has a team. Everyone cares. Or so it seems.

For J, grand final day is sacred, like Christmas, he tells me. For me grand final day represents my inability to fit in. I'm out of step. For a while I tried to care about football, but I felt like a phony so I gave up.

After the grand final is played, I pick up C from his mate's place and J from the pub. It's late and dark. They are both merry. They tell me with huge enthusiasm about the spectacle I have missed. They tell it was a great game. Legendary.

We have friends coming to stay tomorrow. I haven't made beds or defrosted food or caught up in the yards. I leave the boys to sit in front of the fire, watch the replay and argue over umpiring decisions. In the yards I work methodically through the various problems. I'm happy out here in the quiet dark. I'm a visitor, a foreigner, but there's a place for me. I feel the pause my presence causes, all the night things wait. The possums and quolls, wallaby and potoroo. They must watch me come and go. They've learnt I'll only stay for a while and though I'm not a threat, they will wait until I go inside before they creep out.

One of the ewes in the yards has had her eye pecked out by an opportunistic crow. We have a few sheep with only one eye. Amazingly, they adjust and their socket heals well. I loathe the crows in spring, I shake my fist at them as they perch like spectators lining a colosseum, hungry for the wreckage of life. This ewe looks at me with her one remaining eye. Her adopted lamb has hollow flanks and she hasn't let it suck for most of the day, but as soon as I stand next to her she lets it feed. In the quiet dark we stand side by side, she and I, and she tells me she is considering her commitment. Take your time, I say.

When everything is as good as it can be, I walk home. It's black around me and the sky is brilliantly alight. There's a frost settling. The dogs, who sit outside the yards waiting patiently for me to finish, are delighted to be out in the still night. I can hear my labrador snort in the scent of possum, but she's hungry for her dinner so she only scouts an arc of space and does not leave my side.

At the house there are three lambs to feed. C helps me mix up the milk, and then he sits on the couch to give them each a bottle. It's far from a novelty for him. One of the lambs, only hours old, is unbelievably loud. It yells and yells while C feeds the other one. I snap and scream at it – of course it bleats on, oblivious. But I'm uncorked, as if my yelling, the useless irrationality of it, has shocked me to my senses. Sorry, I say to C, and he grins. 'Bit tired, Mum?'

I feed the bleating lamb, put it outside with its skinny mother. The lamb will survive the night, and so will I.

Terry Tempest Williams wrote that when she opened her mother's journals and saw emptiness, she sensed longing. She decided to rewrite that story of longing: create her own story on the empty pages of those journals.

I wonder if the emptiness of being motherless is a longing I am enacting not on the pages of a book but rather on the maimed, disfigured and weak of our flock.

Out in the yards, the black-tagged ewe has turned the corner. My forced feeding of her lamb has caused her hormones to surge and she is mothering him well. Tomorrow I will put her out in the big yard with the other ewes and lambs who have passed through my hands.

When Dana Raphael came up with the word matrescence, she wanted it to echo adolescence, a term and concept we are all familiar with as being an intensely painful period of bewildering hormones, changing bodies, identity shifts and general angst. Sure, some people sail through adolescence with barely a pimple, but most reflect on it as a turbulent time; some, looking back, feel it is hard to know when it started and when it ended.

Imagine if we could extend this generosity of thought to the process of becoming a mother.

Forest raven, *Corvus tasmanicus*, 52–54 cm.
Big, heavy bird with the most massive beak of any of the Australia
corvids,
and shortest tail.
When calling, throat fills out,
but hackles do not form a large, shaggy 'bag'
as in Australian raven (other name is 'crow').
Flight ponderous,
points tail downwards.
Mated pairs hold permanent territories
of 40 hectares.
Non-breeding birds form locally nomadic flocks (up to 100 in
winter in Tasmania).
Voice powerful, deep,
slow, baritone

Korr, korr, (korrrr).

Does not

wail.

Habitat: in Tasmania, ranges from alpine forests/high moors
to wet eucalypt forests, woodlands,
coastal scrubs/beaches, orchards, pine plantations;
adjacent open country in autumn and winter.
(In other words, you cannot go anywhere in Tasmania without
visiting,
however unintentionally,
a family of ravens.)

Nest: large stick nest lined with bark and wool.
Made to a height of 10 m plus in the fork of forest tree.
Eggs: 3–5, blue-green, blotched,
freckled, olive-brown, dark brown, like Australian raven but
slightly larger.
Exceptional parents.

In Australia there are five species of the family Corvidae, plus one introduced. The species are the Australian raven (other name is crow), the forest raven (other name is raven), little raven, Torresian crow and little crow. The house crow (other name is Colombo or Indian crow) is an invasive pest and should be reported and destroyed when identified.

Here in Little Swanport there is just the forest raven, but there are many of them.

What I didn't know before I moved here was that ravens, like cockatoos, are monogamous birds. Their relationships are lifelong, broken only by death. They are also careful parents. They supervise their youngsters and they rarely come to any harm. Notice, when you drive the roads of Tasmania, all the animals killed by passing traffic. Notice the ravens patrolling the edges of the road buffet. The raven mothers and fathers teach their raven babies to hop on and off the road. They show them not to panic, to know that the rushing whoosh of metal and rubber will pass them by as long as they hop off the road. You might see a puff of green feathers of a parrot, or the white striped suit of a silly lapwing, an owl, a magpie, or a tiny cluster of pardalotes, but rarely a raven, black on black.

FOR YEARS, I WORE MY MOTHER'S SILVER NECKLACE and never took it off. It was a beautiful piece, flattened links of silver that lay flush against my throat. It was wildly outside my current circumstances, a piece to treasure. The silver was marked by her life and mine, and when I rubbed it in the fine white sand of the beach where I swim, and drew it out shining and clean, I thought each small mark, each imperfection, made it more beautiful. I wore it so constantly it felt as much a part of me as the skin on the back of my hands. Its clink as I ran, its warmth when I woke in the morning, was a comfort.

I took it off for the first time in my forty-seventh year. What I wore instead was a twenty-dollar piece of whalebone carved in the shape of a humpback's tail, hung on a piece of string. It was given to me by my friend and travelling companion when we went to Tonga on an adventure that dropped from the sky like a benediction. I put it on to show my friend how much I appreciated her gift. Then I left it on while we swam in, sailed upon and paddled through the warm, clear Tongan waters. I liked its roughness. I thought I would take it off when I returned home. But, despite it making me look like a slightly displaced hippie, the whalebone stayed around my neck.

I had travelled to Tonga with my friend to meet up with her sister and husband, who were sailing from the Caribbean back to New Zealand. When I left Tasmania I was winter-white and flabby. That year had not been as bad as the previous for rainfall, but it was close. I left the farm in the final grasp of winter, when it was grey and bare, and flew to a land of vibrant greens, deep blues and warm water. And in the manner of all the best journeys I didn't know what to expect.

Seasickness as it turns out. Eight hours of it on the first sailing leg. I did get my sea legs after that, but they were hard won. Then we landed on a tropical island so magical I felt bewitched. I forgot the nausea. I forgot the winter and all the problems of home. Instead, there was white sand, a reef break at either end of the beach, coconut palms, dogs and roosters and pigs and chickens, fresh fruit and fish curry, and an ocean that was a superhighway for cruising whales. At sunset we sat on the beach nursing a beer and watching a riot of pink and red and molten gold, and the whales breaching and slapping their tails, diving and sending spouts of water like smoke signals into the air. I slept in a tiny beach bungalow and though the ground was firm, on the first night I still moved as if I was riding the sea's back. Tasmania, the kids and J, the dogs and sheep, all seemed to belong to someone else.

The kingdom of Tonga is one of the few places in the world where you can legally swim with whales. As the experience has grown more popular, so have the number of cowboy tour company operators. We heard rumours that boats in the most popular tourist areas were chasing whales, stressing mothers and calves as the operators tried to get their load of swimmers into the water. I was fortunate and this wasn't remotely my experience. Instead, we were the only boat on the water and we were surrounded by whales. We were able to listen, on a hydrophone mic dropped into the water, to the concert of whales singing underneath the boat. We saw clouds of dolphins, and then a whale mother with a calf. Our captain did not approach the mother. He waited, just far enough away to perhaps prick her curiosity. Then, for twenty minutes, maybe half an hour, he seemed to engage her in a conversation. He told us to be ready to get into the water and when we did to just hang there and not swim. We watched as, with the whole ocean at her disposal, the whale turned towards us.

We were over the side of the boat in a second, slipping down into a bottomless blue backlit by sun. Below my fins were more hues of blue, with shafts of sunlight piercing into the depths. And then she was there. And the breath sucked out of me because of the wonder. Her eye locked on us, she was bejewelled and her baby hung as if attached to her back. She didn't swim so much as breathe past us and was gone into the deep. We rose like corks, each of us blasted out of ourselves and almost hysterical with something that fizzed and popped outside words. My friend and I could only gasp and grin. And after that first swim she stayed and played with us, let us hang above her and watch her feeding the calf, her milk like white streamers in the water. When her baby finished feeding, she let us swim beside her, us clumsy humans, desperate not to offend.

We swam with different whales over the next four days, and on the last day we swam once again with the mother and calf. She'd come up beneath us, curious but otherworldly, massive and unknowable. I was on my side, just under the surface, my right arm stretched in front of me, my legs kicking hard, the fins pushing me forward. Her long pectoral fins hung relaxed, only her tail moved – just slightly. I was pulled in and then we were swimming together. In her slipstream I lost my awkwardness, forgot the group, felt weightless, impossibly insignificant and powerful all at once. There was a tugging in me to stay with her. But of course I didn't; I rose to the surface and saw how far I was from the boat and the other swimmers. My fragility returned, I was a land body in the sea, foreign, only a visitor. I lay on my back, surrounded by blue above and below, caught in between worlds.

I wore the whalebone for nine months. It took me back to a place where I shed something, where I jumped into the ocean and was not sure what I would find beneath me, and where I met another mother, outside my understanding, who was curious enough to turn back and swim with me.

A long time after I swam with that mother I heard a story told by a woman describing her teenage self. She was training for an ocean swim. Her morning routine was to ride her bike to the Pacific Ocean off the Californian coast and then swim from the pier to the breakwater and back over, and over, in the dark cusp of dawn. She was training for an open-water race. She'd get out when the sun came up and then cycle home to shower and catch the bus to school.

One morning, she felt a presence in the sea. She described the sensation as the water being hollowed out beneath her. Panic rose. Was it a massive shark swimming with her in the dark? She turned to the shore and saw a man standing under a light on the pier beckoning to her. He was a retired fisherman who worked in the bait shop and often kept an eye on her long training swims. As she trod water the man told her she was swimming with a baby whale. He told her to keep swimming. He told her not to come to shore in case the baby tried to follow her and beached itself or swam off into the giant expanse of ocean beyond the pier. He would put a call out to all the fishing boats and see if anyone had seen its mother.

The young woman kept swimming, so did the baby.

Over the radio came the news that an adult grey whale had been sighted near an oil rig three kilometres off-shore. As if the baby had heard the news, it turned out to sea. The young woman followed it. Now the baby was swimming near the young woman, ahead and just to her side; it was slipstreaming her in the same way its mother would have swum with it. Never had the young woman swum so fast or so effortlessly. Eventually she became tired. The water was cold and she'd been swimming for nearly five hours. The baby would dive down deep and she would tread water and wait until it resurfaced. She decided to turn back. The baby came with her. Then a lifeboat sped towards her and told her the mother whale was less than a kilometre off the pier. The young woman and the baby swam towards the mother.

An adult grey whale is as big as a bus. The young woman became afraid again. The mother came slowly towards them until they were all together. The woman recalled that this reunion was one of the most beautiful things she has ever witnessed. She reached out and touched the mother and then turned and swam back to the beach.

I keep thinking about this story, about how this young woman stayed with the baby, how she did not allow her fear to swamp her senses, how she swam in the slipstream, and she reached out and touched the mother. The woman's name is Lynne Cox and she has gone on to become the greatest-ever open ocean swimmer. When Cox tells the story, she focuses on the lesson she learnt about becoming lost in the ocean. But the story has stayed with me because of Cox's ability to be uncomfortable. She swam with the distressed baby without knowing whether her swimming, her effort, would be to any avail. It's miraculous that it was. Her story is a gift, a reminder that it's only in swimming with the fear, in suspending judgement, that miracles can occur.

My mother, a woman of faith, never received her miracle. My brother never spoke. But out of the ashes of our childhood she gave all three of us the miracle of herself. I wish that for her the price had not been so high.

My eyes are tuned to sheep. The shape of them is in every rock, against the timber, under every bush, behind every tussock.

I see a sheep-shaped mound on the other side of the creek. She is flattened into the creek. I point her out. She's dead, says J. I ask him to stop anyway, and I raise the binos to my eyes. There, against her shoulder, is a tiny lamb. We cross the creek, the tyres spin and then bite on the dry-stone bed. I climb through the fence and pick up the lamb. The ewe is cold, her rear end ravaged. Two eagles circle high above.

The lamb is tiny, too weak to suck. Back at the house I drip colostrum into its mouth and massage its scrawny neck. I wrap it in a towel and lay it by the fire. Later I try again, and with the colostrum fuelling its reflux, it sucks feebly. Next time it will feed more strongly. The instinct grows in the dark.

Laughing kookaburra, *Dacelo novaeguineae*, 41–47 cm.

Big bill pale

below,

crown brown, dark brown ear patch, brown eye, brown wing

mottled pale blue.

Perches watchfully,

makes long sloping glides

onto insects, reptiles, small birds, mammals, crustaceans.

Occasionally plunges into shallow water when hunting and

commonly

when bathing.

In spring, makes high circular display flights

over enemy territory with deep stiff wingbeats.

Voice: famed 'laugh'

staccato

kook-kook-kook rising to shouted *kook-kook-kook-ka-ka-ka*,

slowing to chuckle.

Habitat: woodland, forest clearings, timbered water courses,

farmland, orchards, parks, gardens (everywhere).

Nest: level tree hollow to 20 m high, hole in bank, tree termite

nest, haystack, wall.

Eggs: 2–3, white, roundish.

Range: mainland eastern Australia from Cape York to Eyre

Peninsula.

Introduced Western Australia: 1897.

Tasmania: 1907 (mostly in east and north).

Local grapevine has it that a farmer on the coast shoots kookas on sight. He says they do not belong, they are not native to this place. I do not know when this man's family arrived in Tasmania. But I wonder what length of time he has given himself to claim such gatekeeper status.

Standing in the settling dusk I listen as a kookaburra heralds the end of the day. A tiny bat flies out from under the eaves of the house and traces quick and brilliant patterns over my head. It's so small I think I've imagined it, a fellow resident I did not know we had. It flies, lighter than air, in whirls and giddying circles, loops and bows, and I strain to follow it until it's too dark to see.

LAMBING GOES ON AND ON, and so does feeding. C is home and having him drive for us cuts the jobs in half. One day, hours after we began, I walk back the way we drove. I need to walk, to breathe deeply, move one foot in front of the other instead of the work of lifting, carrying or wrestling sheep. I should be walking through knee-high mixed pastures, rye grass, clover, phalaris – the pasture should be a sea and wind should only make a ripple on its surface. Instead, I'm walking on bare ground.

I have an urgent desire to destock. To let the land wait for the rain, let it hibernate through the hideous dry. We are already running at historically low numbers. In midwinter we'd made the hard decision to sell half our ewes who were scanned in lamb to a terminal sire. It seemed extreme. What if it rained?

It was the right decision. We kept our best sheep, but no rain has come. We can't send lambing ewes on trucks. We can't turn our backs on a lifetime of breeding. So there is no choice. The land has to carry the sheep we have left. But still I wish it was empty, to wait out the dry.

Further up the fence, a lamb I saw when we were feeding is huddled against a post. Possibly its mother planted it in the middle of the paddock while she walked to get a drink, or maybe she's drifted further and further from it while searching for a feed. The tiny thing is exhausted from calling so instead of running from me it just looks. I scoop it up and turn back the way I've come. My wrist hurts. The lamb's heart is pounding. Now I wish I hadn't walked. The house, only a few kilometres away, seems suddenly remote. I put my head down and trudge. I'm so tired and the tiredness has nothing to do with the lamb, or even this walk, but it has everything to do with busyness. There's no time to give C a proper break from school, no time to make the house nice for guests, or for us, no time to read a book, stretch my thoughts into imaginary worlds. The lofty and the banal rub against each other and I know my weariness is because I'm living through a drought. I know that drought is like a great depression.

There was a drought in the year my son turned one.

I was staying with friends and trying to finish my first book. My mother was sick, though we didn't know it yet. I just knew she was so tired and she couldn't keep helping me. My little girl and my baby boy were draining her, and of course she still had my older brother there, too. We went away to give her a break. C was an irrepressible one-year-old, or so he seemed through my grief-strewn vision. He was awake before 5 am, seeming to sense the first lick of light before it could appear in his darkened room. He no longer slept during the day and when he was put to bed in the evening his screams of rage would echo beneath the eaves of the homestead's deep verandas where I was staying. I would set up my computer as far away from him as I could, which happened to be the western closed veranda, and there I'd type while the sweat dripped down my face, in an attempt to finish the edits in what I see now was a sort of madness. It was the second summer of my widowhood, the summer of fishing my son out of pools before he could swim safely, the summer of him climbing out of every and any contraption that sought to hold him in. It was the summer I realised I was unequal to the task of pursuing a career in academia and raising two small children. It was the summer I refused to give in. My wrists ached from being the only parent to lift and swing and wrestle and bathe and dress and catch and put to bed and do it all again in the morning.

My body holds memories in ways I don't understand. The aching in my wrists as I carry this lamb has called up that deep-in-my-bones weariness. It was there in the intake of breath as I bent to pick up the lamb and instead felt my son's thrashing, resistant body.

Lambing officially finishes today though we may have a few more late ones. I don't have a ewe I can graft this lamb on to and I don't want another orphan to raise. If I leave it, there's a strong chance it'll just drift in front of the wind until it blows against a tussock or a fence post. Yet I turn and walk into the wind carrying it. I'll take it up to the mob of ewes and lambs.

I'm drenched in motherhood, in the act of birthing. All going well I'm more than halfway through my allotted years. My mother has been dead for nearly sixteen years but I'm still living in the framework she gave me. Carrying the lamb, I wonder how tempted she was to abandon us, to abandon her eldest child. I wonder how hard she fought against it. She didn't walk away and so here am I, not walking away.

I'm not sentimental about the lambs. I do not *love* them. I do not keep them alive because I think they're cute. It's something much deeper than that. When I see instinct at work – a ewe rushing back to find her lamb, pushing against her desire to flee, to follow her mob, to be absorbed, invisible, acting against one instinct to follow another – or when I see a newborn lamb learn to breathe, and stand and walk and follow its mother, all within minutes of being born, something in me flutters.

Is it hope?

If this wind dropped, this lamb I'm carrying might stand a chance. I've walked as far as I can without causing chaos and perhaps mismothering other new lambs. I put it down and kick it forward towards the ewes. It looks in the right direction, takes some steps towards its mob and I back out of its line of sight and walk home. I'm light and my wrists hum.

Later, just on dusk, to placate me C drives with me to the lookout hill to see if the lamb has been abandoned again. We sit up there and take turns looking through the binoculars. What's spread before us is a study in spareness. The paddocks are brown, the pink in the sunset softened not by green but by the dust kicked up by ewes trekking to muddy waterholes to drink at the end of yet another day without rain. The poplar trees should be a riot of fluorescent green. The gums should be tipped with new growth. Instead, what green I can see is dull and desperate.

We are watchers being watched. Two sea eagles on a branch of a dead tree look over us. The tree is so old it might as well be made of iron. In our winds, often heavy with salt, it will last longer than iron. The eagles, in their white and grey, are ghostly, spectral. I wonder what we look like to them. I know the shift in perspective would show me something essential. Something I can't see from down here. Is my labour pointless? Is that what I would see?

Sitting next to my teenage son I feel the prickle of time passing. It runs across the back of my neck, down my arms and through my fingers. Further up the valley are two trees black with crows. The noise is a violence. C and I take turns watching through the binoculars. A ewe stamps her front feet, then lowers her head and charges at a crow who hops too close to her newborn lamb. It's only her fierceness that keeps her lamb from harm. She's got nothing else. No teeth or talons. No poison. No hard hooves. No bulk. Just a mother's ferocity.

I'm surrounded with these stories of negotiating life. What if today hadn't been windy – would that lamb have left the spot on which its mother planted it? What if I surrender to the spiralling possibilities, if I let life roll over me and, instead of resisting death, accept that to witness the arbitrariness of nature has its own power?

*

By the end of spring, despite our hard work the lambing percentages are woeful. The drought has won. But we're still here. We buy a load of water for a dam. The garden is dead. Everything is weak and hungry and we still have the heat of summer ahead of us. I send Belle, our old thoroughbred mare, off to friends in the north of the state, who at least have a pick of grass. I've been feeding her grain and precious hay but she needs grass to put flesh over her ribs, to give a gloss to her dull coat. We have deer grazing in the garden at night. They are eating the pot plants, which ridicules the effort I take to save water from the washing, the shower, the sink to water them. When I go out walking I keep the dogs close. The wallabies they once would have chased without a hope of catching are now so weak that even the corgis can hunt one down. I hear about it raining in other places. We sell the lambs straight off their mothers. Someone with grass will make a big profit.

I wish I had a scale, a finely tuned set of definitions on what drought is, so we could measure it, so we could see when we have reached that which can't be borne.

Since I moved here nine years ago there has never been a late summer rain, nor an autumn break. I could list the rain figures for you but most likely, unless you're a climate scientist or a farmer, they won't mean much. So, better to take you by the hand and ask you to stand with me beside the creek while I introduce you, rock by rock, dry hole to bleached earth, bare ground to dead trees. This is what a drought looks like. If you stand with me here, you'll see a sheep bogged in mud, desperate for a drink, but there's nothing for it to drink and it's too weak to drag its limbs to hard earth. You'll see a roo stand and watch us walk by, too weak to thump its tail and hop away.

It will rain. Though I find my faith lacking on this, J believes it. He says it always has before. And I think, yes, it always has, and perhaps it will again – but what about the time after it rains? What about when we are back here again? Every sensible person can see the climate of our seasons is changing. There will be a new generation of farmers who will learn how to farm in response. But any response has to speak of the pain of drought. We need to remember drought when it does rain. We need to remember the naked ground under the swaying grass. To change, we need to remember the pain, but to go on we need to let it go.

summer

Words that are useful to know

PETRICHOR (NOUN)

You may not know the word but you'll know the smell. It's the tingle in the back of your nose, the intoxicating scent of hot ground after rain. It was coined by two Australian scientists who persisted in experimenting with rocks to find out what elements created this distinctive smell. They blasted the rocks to rid them of any chemicals. They discovered that all that was required to produce the scent was a little wetness on organic matter. *Petri* from the Greek meaning 'stone', and *ichor* meaning 'blood of the gods'.

SOUTHERN BOOBOOK, *Ninox novaeseelandiae*, 29 cm.
Over twenty common names,
most of which mimic
its breathy two-toned call.
Morepork, mopoke, ruru.
Widespread small brown owl with suggestion of large, pale-rimmed
'goggles' bordering dark patch around each eye.
Smaller than its mainland cousins, with bright yellow eyes (like a
tiger's hide).
Roosts by day in thick foliage.
Disturbed, slips silently out until mobbed by small birds.
Watch for them at dusk when they sit silent on exposed branches,
fence posts
until they launch to catch flying insects, moths or small birds in
mid-air,
or pounce on spiders, mice
and scuttling warm things.
Voice: well known, quick, falsetto
morepork,
repeated; also (listen carefully) falsetto
yo-yo-yo-yo. Near nest they make a noise like a cat, *brrrwow*, and low,
mor-mor-mor-mor, on and on and on.
Young birds trill.
Habitat: rainforests to mallee, dense mulga; margins of almost
treeless plains; woodlands; lightly timbered farming country;
pine forests, orchards, parks, gardens; street-trees including leafy,
exotic poplars, elms, willows, cypresses
(erupts into cereal-growing areas in mouse plagues).

Breeds: August–December.
Nest: on decayed wood debris,
in a tree-hollow.
Eggs: 2–3, white, rounded.

THE MOON IS FULL AND THE AIR warm enough to have the heavy door onto the veranda open. I lie in bed and listen to moths battering the thin glass of the window. They sound like rain. And then that sound – *more-poke, more-poke.* The little owl on silent wings is hunting. I imagine the scuttle of mouse and bat, or a trail of moths rising to the light of the moon. And the thrill of the bird launching itself through the darkness.

The paredarerme people of the south-east nation of lutruwita/trouwunna, on whose country I live and work, say in the beginning women rose from the sea carrying their children, men fell to the earth from the stars and everyone came from the sky. Kinship between the people, the land, the animals, the plants, the sea and sky is the thread that links them in place. This idea, of a mutual caring, a thread sewing us into the country, is something I keep returning to; it's something I want to understand. But it's complicated. My belonging still has the feeling of a theft.

In her revolutionary book *Braiding Sweetgrass: Indigenous Wisdom, Scientific Knowledge, and the Teachings of Plants*, the American writer, scientist, healer and activist Robin Wall Kimmerer describes standing on a high bluff on the Pacific north-west coast. She looks to the east and sees the hills are a ragged range of clear-cut forests, and to the south is an estuary dammed and dyked, which means no salmon will ever make their way to their traditional breeding grounds. Out to sea she watches a bottom-dragging trawler scrape the ocean floor, and far away to the north, beyond her mortal eyes, she knows the earth is being torn up for oil. 'Against the backdrop of that history, an invitation to settler society to become indigenous to place feels like a free ticket to a housebreaking party.' Immigrants, she says, cannot by definition be indigenous.

How then, immigrant and indigenous, do we move forward?

For Kimmerer the way forward is to look to nature. She gives us *Plantago major*, the common plantain. Its Latin epithet *Plantago* refers to the sole of the foot. The plant became known as White Man's Footstep. She explained the ways plantain has an ability to colonise compacted and disturbed soils. It survives being trampled and has spread all over the world. She lists its uses, its fresh young leaves could be eaten, and its mature leaves when cooked in stews released essential calcium and beta-carotene. Its seeds could be pounded to make flour. Its roots were used to treat fevers and respiratory illnesses. Young leaves were made into poultices for burns, wounds, and to take the sting out of insect bites. The tough fibres in the mature plant can be made into cords, fishing lines or even sutures. Kimmerer writes, 'It's a foreigner, an immigrant, but after five hundred years of living as a good neighbour, people forget that kind of thing. Being naturalised to place means to live as if this is the land that feeds you, as if these are the streams from which you drink, that build your body and spirit. To become naturalised is to know that your ancestors lie in this ground.'

My mother's ashes are buried in the country of her childhood and mine. Where they lie is not in our family anymore, and the thought can torture me if I let it. But hearing the morepork's call unpeels me from this time and place and moves me back there. The call is a sound of safety, a shortcut to a place where I was held in the blessings of kinship. I was too young to understand that the country was not mine to love. Instead, I gave myself to it wholeheartedly. Now I am older and I see that the sense of place I carry is more complicated.

The Irish philosopher and poet John O'Donohue spoke about a place within us all that he calls an inner sanctuary. In his poem 'Beannacht', which is the Gaelic word for 'blessing', O'Donohue conjures an image of a soul burdened by grief and loss. His murmured prayer to me, to us, is that when we stumble, the earth will move beneath us so we are held, that when we are lost the moon will shine a path for us to follow. He writes of the power of our ancestors rising to protect us, and the colours of the drawing-in of the day that will appear to delight. His poem conjures the natural world as our protector, as a reflection of the beauty of the inner sanctuary within us all. He is willing me to see how the beauty around me reflects that hidden part within. So the morepork of one place is mirrored in this other and if I am generous and gentle I may receive the blessing of them both.

Clouds that are useful to know

Cirrus (hair)
Cumulus (a heap)
Stratus (layer)
Nimbus (rain-bearing)

In among the three- and four-year-old ewes, I see what might be a prolapse, but after watching the ewe through the binos for a few minutes I think it is a set of hind legs poking from her backside. A breech, I say, and hand J the binos. That'd be right, he mutters.

He manages to cut the ewe from the back of the mob, but she's strong and fast. She's heading for the bush right on the boundary. On the other side of the fence are one hundred acres of our neighbour's out-of-control gorse. J swings the ute across the ewe's path and once again I leap from the door. My fingers catch her wool, but she busts past me straight into the bush and disappears.

We'll never find her in there, J says. He has a meeting in town. We have to go.

The ewe with the breech lamb gnaws at me. I hope she might have been able to get the lamb birthed. I think if she has gone down I might find her again and catch her. I drive back, cross the creek, put the ute into low ratio and nose forward through thick bush. In a good season it is impossible to get in here. But this year, though it's rough, I'm not scared of getting bogged. We are not far from the highway but I feel like I've entered a different realm. A little edge of wildness. Dusty is on the back of the ute on a short chain. I can see her mouth open, she's tasting the scent of roo. She whines and I tap the back window, then she sits, quietly contrite at her lack of control. We follow the line of the creek until I can't push through the bush anymore. I leave the ute and walk.

It takes me a while to realise I'm staring straight at the ewe. She's standing in a thick grove of wattles, her perfect stillness the only real camouflage. Now I realise something. I came back hoping not to find her. But there she is and her presence demands that I must act. I stand in the conundrum of this moment. I decide my best chance is to push her gently back onto the boundary fence and hope I can work her into a corner.

I take a step or two closer, increasing the pressure. She backs through the wattle and onto the fence. I move to my left and trip on a hidden log. I take my eyes off her – only for a second, but when I look again to where she was, there is only bush. She is gone. Swallowed. I don't move, scanning, hoping she'll flick an ear or make some small movement to draw my gaze to her. But she doesn't and the space feels empty. In the end I walk up to where I last saw her but there's no trace of a sheep. I don't understand how she pushed through the thick bush without making a cascade of sound. I spend the next hour waiting and watching. I search that section of fence line, push up and down into places no sheep would go. I can find no trace of her. I have to admit defeat. It's getting late. The forest is her fortress and she will either have her lamb in there and lead it out to rejoin the mob or she'll die and her flesh and bones will be eaten by devils. Anything left of her after they have finished will be carried off by ants and there will be nothing, except my memory of our meeting.

THE MAYO CLINIC DEFINES APHASIA as a condition that removes the ability to communicate. 'It can affect the ability to speak, write and understand language, both verbal and written … The severity of aphasia depends on a number of conditions, including the cause and the extent of the brain damage.'

Aphasia can be treated with speech and language therapy; by relearning and practising language skills and other means of communication. Family members can participate in these therapies.

But what if you have never communicated? What if your brain damage happened at birth, or soon after birth? What if there is no language there to be found?

When I was a little girl I imagined my brother unlocked. I imagined the adventures we would have. I imagined the conversations. I imagined everyone's surprise when they met him after his unlocking. The miracle of it. And it seemed all I had to do was believe hard enough and he would be set free. My faith would be the catalyst. I kept waiting for it to happen. Him, deep below the surface, quietly buried; me waiting for the moment he would emerge from the boy who bit and scratched, screeched and shat.

I'm thinking of frogs, of the burrowing frog in particular, and how they live beneath the earth for years, in ground so hard you might strike it with a pickaxe and the mark you make would be as small as a comma on a page. Those frogs may stay deep in the earth, sometimes as deep as two metres, for decades. I imagine them as sleeping beauties, sealed off from the trauma above. I imagine the rains coming, the thrill of the first molecule of moisture reaching their living coffins, their slow ascent to the surface, the wild cacophony of life they join. Can a frog feel joy? I believe it would.

In an essay, the writer Robert Macfarlane asks, 'Does it matter that a powerful navigational device has been added to our cyborg lives?' He's talking about our phones, the glowing blue dot on our maps signifying our location on the earth. Macfarlane trips through some fascinating examples of how animals and birds find their way. He starts off with the image of a limpet inching its way across a rock, then looks at the Arctic tern, which travels from Greenland to Antarctica and back, some 64,000 kilometres. He describes the great vertical migration of plankton, which rise to the surface of the sea at twilight and sink back to the deep at sunrise. And how bees, blind by human standards, spend hours flying from bloom to bloom, haphazardly, yet when they return to the hive they fly the shortest possible distance and, on their return, they *dance* to communicate where they have been to the other bees. Macfarlane argues that 'our remarkable navigational ability is closely connected to our ability to tell stories about ourselves that unfold backwards and forwards in time'. I agree, but, individually, our navigational ability is pretty meagre compared to that of a single caribou, or a salmon or limpet. As a species we've found our way to the moon and we've crisscrossed the oceans and skies. And yet so many of us are foreigners in the country we live on. We can't find our way without our phones. We have become captives to the devices that are meant to set us free.

My brother could not speak, but he could walk. In walking he was telling stories. When he ran away we would ask, where have you been? And he would ignore us, or grow angry and shove us. I see my small self, incandescent with rage at yet another moment hijacked by him. WHERE have you been? And he would turn from me, his face hurt that I would ask of him something he could not give.

In Tasmania, to my great delight I have met a small group of women who love to walk. With them I've explored some wild and empty country. We've trekked in the south-west and made our way for days across trackless country following a compass bearing. We've slogged our way through vertical scrub, lost in a world of tea tree, once more trusting the compass, for we couldn't see beyond our faces. We've walked up peaks and along beaches so wild that if a wave knocked you over you would be swept out to sea in an instant. We've walked for days without seeing another soul. We've been caught high on a ridge when a weather system rolled in and have sat huddled together behind a rock sharing a hot drink and waiting out the worst of the storm, then crawled off the ridge because the wind was so strong it kept knocking us off our feet.

All of us are in the middle of our lives. Jobs, children, partners, responsibilities. The walking releases us from these things and in planning and executing the treks we become something else – more selfish and attentive. We put our packs on our backs and carry literal weight; it's a relief to drop the metaphorical. With these women I've been reunited with myself. Walking for me is truth-telling, a place I go where my body speaks so my voice doesn't have to. I walk to know and be known.

I think we have forgotten how it feels not to know exactly where we are. Not long ago I was walking on Flinders Island. I was there to write a story about the island. The shack I was staying in looked out across a long stretch of beach and up to Mount Killiecrankie. I set off to climb the mountain on a bright blue morning. I put a pear in my pocket, tied a jacket round my waist and carried my water bottle. It was a beautiful walk. I met a couple up the top who said they were doing a circuit. They had hiking boots, day packs, walking poles. I love a circuit. I instantly decided to scrap my plan to walk back the way I'd come; instead I would walk the track they'd described, down to the beach below and then along the coast and back up the four-wheel drive track to where my car was parked.

I headed off down the mountain fast so I could swim in the bay on my own. The water was bracing and clear and afterwards I lay on the warm rocks and ate my pear. I walked up the first headland and found some pink surveyors tape marking a track, or what I thought was the track. I headed off. Within minutes of entering the bush I saw two snakes. The bush thickened up. The pink tape was less obvious. I was closer to the imposing cliffs above than the coast. I'd obviously come off the track the couple had talked about. But I was heading in the right direction and I could hardly get lost. I muttered aloud, 'Keep the sound of the waves on your left'; surely I would walk out of the bush. I didn't know how long the circuit was. I hadn't looked at a map. No one knew where I was. I told myself to be careful and not fall over, not get bitten by a snake. I comforted myself – I could just turn around, there is plenty of daylight. I am *not* lost. The thick bush continued. Suddenly there was a small clearing and what looked like craters in the ground – later I found out they were meant to be nuclear-fallout bunkers, dug by a man struggling with madness who, decades ago, lived at the bottom of the cliffs. I kept walking. Twice I almost turned back. Twice I told myself not to be ridiculous, to hold my nerve. I pushed through thick tea tree. There was no track. I searched for another rotting piece of pink tape. I wasn't lost, I just couldn't see where I was going.

Logic prevailed and, after two hours in thick tea tree, I found a track. Oh, the relief of it. It was overgrown, unused, and I pushed through the bush until I found a sheltered bay – and in it I washed off the heat of the walk, the prickle of fear that had made my mouth dry. Back at the car I looked at my phone, which for much of the way had been nothing more useful than a camera. It told me I'd walked fourteen kilometres.

I love walking alone. But I realise I'm used to following a track, it's my anchor. It pulls me along. But this day, walking on my own, no mobile reception, no path on the earth, cracked open the rustiness of my wayfaring self. It was a good muscle to exercise. The metaphor of the thick bush. The trusting of my forward movement. The faith to commit and not turn around. The dry-mouthed fear. All of it was a physical expression of me.

The year my son leaves, the year I am writing this book, my friends and I decide to walk the Larapinta Trail out of Alice Springs. It's a big deal for us to leave Tassie, but we manage to coordinate ourselves. We (that is, not me) organise a four-wheel drive to pick us up from Alice Springs Airport and drop us out on a trailhead, from where we will follow the Larapinta Trail for six days and walk back into Alice. We are six middle-aged women. We feel reckless and open. The first night we camp on the soft sand of a creek bed. We light a fire to cook our dinner. The flames leap into the night sky. A ridge of red rock shelters us and the sky is alight with a million stars. Impulsively we stand together and turn our backs to the fire. We speak out loud and ask permission to walk out tomorrow. We say to the starlit night that we are from Tasmania; we say we will walk with respect and love in our hearts.

Barry Lopez writes of his goal in walking over country – it is to access an intimacy with place. He uses the word love. We do too.

The next day and the next we walk on ridges, along creek beds, across spinifex plains and up red rock mountains. We walk through clouds of emerald-coloured budgerigars, through mists of chattering finches. We make each other laugh, we tell stories and camp beneath the ghost gums. Unlike the walks we do in Tasmania, we see other walkers and the track is clearly marked. Yet I still feel that we are finding our way. It has rained in the weeks before and the creek holes are full. We are respectful of the holes marked 'No swimming', but we come across one hole that is dark and deep. We strip and clamber over slippery rocks to lower ourselves into the cold water. When I get out of the waterhole I let the heat of the sun dry the mineral blessings onto my skin. We continue on the track, but something has changed. It's us. I can see it in the faces of these women I know. Each of us will carry forward an imprint of this walk. We have received this expanse of sky, this scope of rock. We've walked with humility in the face of a place we do not understand.

Grey fantail, *Rhipudura fuliginosa*, 14–17 cm.
Nickname: cranky fan.
Grey with short white eyebrows;
white mark behind eye; white tips to wing-coverts;
white throat and whisker-mark;
dark (sooty) breast-band; underparts white.
Outer feathers of dark grey fantail are edged,
or perhaps broadly tipped white,
or perhaps
wholly white (according to where the cranky fan lives).
Singles, pairs, open companies.
Switches, spreads tail;
swoops, loops, stunts, dives after flying insects.
Forages in foliage (as high as 30 m or more)
joins feeding *associations*
(thornbills, pardalotes and suchlike).
Voice: sharp
dek;
sweet, tinny, animated fiddle-like song, *ascending*, ending in
drawn-out, rising,
silvery notes.
Nest: beautiful small grey cup
tailed like a wine glass without a base,
of fine grass, bark strips, plant fibre,
spider web.
In slender horizontal fork of shrub or tree, low to 12 m.
Eggs: 2–3; yellowish or fawn-white,
spotted light brown, rufous, grey.

We do not agree on many things, J and I. And when life is tense he brings me bird nests he finds in the paddocks, blown down from their high perch, caught in a thicket of gorse, abandoned by the bank of the creek. Each of them is a work of art. He places them in my hand like an offering, an olive branch, a spider's gossamer thread that reaches me, and I am softened.

On a windowsill, catching dust, is my collection of nests. Goldfinch, blackbird and, most perfect of all, grey fantail.

When I first came here I resented the cranky, creaky little bird. On my walks it would chide me from the gorse, or swoop in dramatic stunts like a high-wire walker from the gums outside the cottage, or tease me from the fence line. I wanted it to be something else. I wanted me to be someone else.

His cousin, willie wagtail, *Rhipidura leucophrys*, lives in every place in Australia except southern Tasmania. Willies and I go way back. When I go to the mainland one always finds me soon after I arrive and I bow and thank it for welcoming me. But down here, in the *one little bit* of the whole of Australia where there are no willies, there is an abundance of his little grey cousin, the cranky fan. Even his name, cranky fan, feels unfriendly compared to the willie wagtail. Who would you take to the ball: the grey fantail or the willie wagtail? I do that thing, the comparison thing. I think, his suit is not so crisply pressed, he does not sweetly serenade me with his song when I can't sleep, he does not know me and my ghosts, he does not swoop into my dreams and lead me back in time. I think, his eyebrows are not a thing of wonder and his whiskers are a bit short. I think, how will I learn to love him?

I understand why the English brought their birds, their blackbirds and skylarks. The impulse to join our separate selves, to make the break a smoothing-over, not to talk of the scar, is always there. But I also understand this world is not a passive place. It will not stand back and have an imprint of somewhere else placed over its bones. Blackbirds and skylarks are different here. They are changed by their new home.

And besides, one day willie did visit me down here. It was just after my father died. I was making a pie, washing sheets and remaking beds. I was sweeping the floor. I was making a home. And willie dropped in. I heard him through the little window in the stone kitchen and thought I had left my senses. I ran outside and there he was, perched on the garden fence scolding me, calling me out. Hello! I said. Don't go, I said, please stay. Look around, it's lovely here. No cats (as if such a thing would worry him). Mosquitoes as fat as wrens, I said. And me. I'm here. Please stay, I said.

And he did. For three days he appeared every time I stepped outside. Then he left and I felt lonely all over again.

It's taken me almost a decade to learn to look past willie to see the cranky fan. I'm learning to greet him as I step out the back door. Learning to love him popping up on my walks. Learning to marvel at his aerial stunts, his daredevil antics fifty metres above my head. Learning to hear his silver trill as it slides up the scale, his murmured greeting *dek dek* said to me in apparent disapproval.

Above the oak's sculpted branches a cranky fan flits and flutters. I stand and crane my neck. He is drawing for me, the spirit of the tree rising.

ONCE, WHEN I WAS MUCH YOUNGER, I went on an adventure to Alaska. We, my husband and I, loaded a month's worth of food into a kayak and set off with ten other adventurers to paddle Prince William Sound. We pushed our kayaks off the beach at the little town of Whittier. The town, whose smallness I recognised, sat perched between the sea and steeply rearing mountains. The savage contours emphasised how far we were from home. As we paddled away it started to rain. It was soft, a greeting, an exchange; it was moisture without intent, as if we were merely passing through a cloud. But that was just the beginning. For the next fourteen days it never stopped. What I didn't know, what I didn't understand as we set off, was that I was about to be schooled in the art of rain.

The drought broke on the east coast of Tasmania when I knew it would never rain again.

In the dawn of the first rain, I went out. In disbelief I walked across the creek, there was a movement there, of rocks wet, a hint of something to come as if the rain overnight had awoken it, had whispered *be ready*. The creek was still just a tongue of foetid water, a word that leapt from rock to bare rock, in a place I would once have swum. I stood on its bed. In its heart. Raised my arms above my head and imagined the volume of water required to fill this thirsty land.

I kept walking through rain. The world was swelling, where just yesterday – hours ago, really – the land had been light with dust. Now I walked and it felt different, portent and slippery. I walked to the top of the hill and stood beneath a very old tree. I placed my hands on its trunk and felt its pulsing want. It pushed up into the sky, and under my feet its roots reached through the dry ground and opened themselves, too. Under my hand it shook and I felt humbled by my lack of faith.

On Prince William Sound the rain did not cease. I came to think that I could not exist if I was not known by rain. I came to see that I could not shelter from it, hide from it, wait for it to pass; that instead I must live in it and accept it. My hands become swollen with it, my skin puckered by it. Each night we would pitch our camp on the side of the Sound in the small space between the forest and the water on the rocky shore. We would rig our tents and string a slight piece of nylon tarp between the trees. Beneath the thin shelter we would hunker down in our waterproof clothes and cook our meal as the rain poured from the sky and the sea lapped at our feet. I ceased to be able to imagine 'dry'. After eating I would wash our dishes at the sound's edge, use the pebbles to scrub them, then rinse them in the rising tide. I would fill my water bottle by tipping a corner of the tarp into the wide mouth. I'd climb into the soft green dripping forest, pull my wet clothes down and squat. The shock was always in standing and pulling my wet clothes over clammy, chilled skin.

Waiting for me in our sodden tent was the one thing I managed to keep dry – my sleeping bag. Protecting it from the rain was my life's mission. I would take every wet piece of clothing off before I got into it at night. In the morning I would stuff it into two thick garbage bags and then its stuff-sack and finally into a waterproof packing bag. Buried deep in it was a pair of dry socks. The sleeping bag and the socks were the only truly dry things I owned. Every night I would strip and crawl into the dry sleeping bag and find the socks and pull them over my cold, swollen feet.

This wet world was something I had never experienced. It was something outside of my imagination. My sleeping bag was sanity. I could stand all the things the day threw at me if I had a dry sleeping bag to crawl into at the end of it. It didn't matter what else happened in the day, what the weather did, or how my fellow adventurers reacted, I had a safe, dry place. A thin nylon shell stuffed with feathers, a bulwark against the all-consuming wet.

It rained for fourteen days without even the smallest hole in the weather. We lived in a steady beat of water. I stopped believing it would ever stop raining; I gave in to living in a cloud of water.

I think of that time so often. It seems like a fairy tale, that it could rain that much.

There was another time. A few years later: I was a mother and we lived in Vancouver. I was studying, trying to juggle an embryonic career, a child and a husband. We lived right on the edge of a thousand-acre Douglas fir forest and in September it started raining and it did not stop for nine months. I forgot what heat was. I forgot my childhood studies in brown, in dust. We'd left a southern hemisphere winter and arrived in a northern summer and in truth the temperatures did not feel that different. People played and ate and lived outside with a desperation I recognised but didn't understand. I was told the rain would come to stay and I didn't believe them. But it did just that. One day the skies were blue and cloudless, the next the rain came and stayed in all its forms. Everything was wet and stayed wet. The people accepted it, adapted. I spent the months in shock, as I had in the fourteen days of rain on Prince William Sound, that rain could exist like that.

I know rain as an event. I know it as something to be treasured, something to be feared, but not as a season. Now rain is so rare I don't want to be away from home if it's forecast. I want to lie in bed and listen to the patter on the roof. I want to step into the garden and have the smell of it hit me like a drug. Mostly my life here has been about waiting for rain.

The drought breaks, as most do, in stages. That first rain brought an awful flood that swept away fences and left scars in the bare ground where precious topsoil had once been. The one blessing was that we did not lose stock, but to watch the farm flow out to sea on the broad back of floodwater after years of looking for rain made our hearts sick. And all the phone calls – 'You got rain!' 'Yes,' we said. Yes. And we tried to hide the bitterness at what it had done.

The water sank and J, C and I worked to clear the debris. We burnt the rubbish and with each day the blow from the flood was softened by a growing fuzz of green.

In the aftermath of the flood I spend hours dragging logs and sticks and clumps of gorse into piles and setting them alight. I rake the flood debris from fences. I pick up sticks and make pyres out of them and though the flood has gouged wounds into our beautiful flats the green is starting to work a healing on us all.

And then it came to be that we needed more rain and just when we were braced to go back into drought, an astonishment, a huge soft easterly settled over our heads and the deep caves under the creek were filled and weeks and then months after the first big rain, we had more and more and the creek was full. The ground was soft and we began to hope.

Epilogue

IT KEPT RAINING. It rained through autumn and winter as we were all ordered to stay home. By the time spring arrived the paddocks were covered in a thick blanket of clover.

J brings all the mobs in to give them a pre-lamb drench. When he returns for lunch he's battered. The ewes are so strong, he says. He pulls Doris, the one with the dodgy hip, out of her mob, and another ewe who has big teats, and puts them in the paddock behind the yards so we can check them. The ewe with the swollen udder becomes known as Dolly.

When the lambing starts in earnest, we hold our breath. As each day rolls into the next with no problems we begin to look forward to the run. We sit on the hill and peer through the binos. Everywhere we look there are healthy, strong lambs on the ground. We get more rain. There are no abandoned lambs, no weak ewes.

Dolly has twins and I bring her into the yards. There is no way the lambs are going to be able to suck off her misshapen, swollen teats. I milk her and get the lambs going. It takes a few days but her udder settles down and the lambs learn to suck. She's a good mother and her lambs grow quickly.

J comes home one morning and says he thinks Doris has started to lamb. We check her at lunchtime and she has not made much progress. Let's get her in, I say. Walking behind her, I hope we haven't let her go too long before helping her. I'm stricken with tension. We catch her and J pulls her lamb.

I'm holding her head. 'Is it alive?' I ask. Laughing, he says, it sure is. We step back and watch the miracle of birth. The lamb shakes its head as Doris's rough tongue goes to work. She is muttering to the lamb, the threat of us forgotten. For the next few days she doesn't move. She waits for me to bring her a dipper of sheep pellets, but she doesn't need them – the grass is thick around her. The lamb is another ripper. I put Dolly and Doris out in the paddock together.

The weeks roll on. It is the best lambing we have ever had. No orphans. No lambs on the bottle. No reluctant mothers. No foster babies.

Everything is fat and well fed. There is so much grass. The only things that are hungry are the eagles, devils and crows.

On our rounds we come upon a ewe who has just given birth. Her lamb is standing on wobbly legs. Beside her in the grass is a wedge-tailed eagle. It is eyeball to eyeball with the ewe. She does not move. The bird opens its wings, making itself even bigger. She shifts so her body is between the lamb and the bird. A hundred metres away is the main mob of ewes. We drive across the paddock slowly. The bird sees us and as we keep coming it takes a few steps then flaps its huge wings and lifts into a dead tree on the boundary of the paddock. The ewe walks slowly towards the mob, her new lamb pressed against her side.

In *Braiding Sweetgrass*, Robin Wall Kimmerer asks, 'What does a good mother do when mothering time is done?'

I walk the ridges and rejoice in the fresh flushes of lichen on the rocks, in the tinge of fluorescent green pushing out from the tall gums. The dogs run on and I pass through a swollen, gurgling world. We arrive at the second-biggest creek. The dogs plunge in. They swim in circles of gulping delight. I'm still astounded, speechless at this transformation. Stones that have stood bare to the sun for years are now deep under water. I take my boots off, roll up my jeans to wade through the crossing; and then I pause and watch the dogs. They are swimming in the deep hole simply for joy. They could be like me and pick their way across the shallow water, but they have plunged in. They swim across and then around the pool, their tongues taste the water, they are drunk on delight and I watch as they reach the other side and haul themselves out, shake and then leap into the rough sand and green shoots and roll and roll. These old dogs, old ladies – well, two of them – gambol as if they have swum in an elixir of youth.

I bend down. I take off my beanie. My fingerless gloves. I take off my coat, my jumper and shirt, pull my boots and stand in my woollen socks while I peel off my jeans and undies and bra and finally my socks. I stand and let the wind prick my flesh. Then I walk into the water.

It's as cold as a mountain top and full against my skin. My lungs splutter in shock and then relax. I take a breath and dive down. Pulling into the deep, I feel my ears pop and hold myself in the clear silence as I push down, seeking the stones I've walked on for years. My hands are above my head and I am neither touching earth nor sky – suspended in life.

When I surface the dogs go wild with applause. They are so happy I've joined them. I swim to the edge of the creek and as I get out my back is straighter. Standing in the pale warmth of the spring sun, I let the water dry on me: I want it in me, I want my body to absorb the miracle. To know this water is my saviour. There's no one to see me and yet my need is seen.

When I'm dry I pull my clothes back on and we walk home.

To my children

Works Cited

This book stands on a library. Here are the foundation stones that appear in the text:

George Adams, *The Complete Guide to Australian Birds*, Viking, Sydney, 2018.

Lynne Cox, 'Off Course, Act 2, Synchronised Swimmers', *This American Life*, episode 765, March 2022.

Robin Wall Kimmerer, *Braiding Sweetgrass: Indigenous Wisdom, Scientific Knowledge, and the Teaching of Plants*, Milkweed Editions, Minnesota, 2013.

Barry Lopez, *Arctic Dreams: Imagination and Desire in a Northern Landscape*, Scribner, New York, 1986.

Barry Lopez, 'Love in a Time of Terror: on natural landscapes, metaphorical living and Warlpiri identity', *Orion Magazine*, August 2020.

Helen Macdonald, *Vesper Flights: new and collected essays*, Jonathan Cape, London, 2020.

Robert Macfarlane, 'The Landscapes Inside Us', *New York Review of Books*, 1 July 2021.

Graham Pizzey and Frank Knight, *The Field Guide to the Birds of Australia*, HarperCollins, Sydney, 2001.

Terry Tempest Williams, *When Women Were Birds, Fifty-Four Variations on Voice*, Picador, New York, 2012.

Terry Tempest Williams, *Erosion: Essays of Undoing*, Sarah Crichton Books, Farrar, Straus & Giroux, New York, 2019.

Acknowledgements

It seems entirely fitting to write these acknowledgments to the beat of steadily falling rain. Through my window it drifts over a garden dressed in riotous, outrageous greens. When I was keeping the lambing diaries, around which *Graft* is based, I could not imagine this season of abundance. A memoir, written in a landscape of bare dirt, dry creek beds and empty dams and published in a world of flooding rivers, bogged tractors and thick, grass-covered paddocks emphasises the extremes farmers are facing in producing fibre and food in an era of accelerating climate change. To catch a fragment of our shared experience was the impulse behind *Graft* and none of these fragments would have been possible without the network of people who support me.

Jim, thank you for making room for me in this beautiful place. The hours we've spent on lambing runs, passing the binoculars, arguing about what we are looking at, watching birds, catching ewes, pulling lambs; and then in the yards, drafting, pushing up, sorting out, wrangling are the bedrock of this book. I hope I've captured something of our life together.

Alison Clark, your gift of our Tuesday sessions is also at the heart of this book. Talking to you peeled something from my eyes and I saw what was in front of my face. Thank you for your generosity, time and wisdom.

Bernadette Brennan, what if we hadn't met all those years ago at Sydney University teaching bored American exchange students Australian Studies? You with your brilliant, demanding teenage daughters, me newly widowed, pregnant and with a fairy of a five-year-old, both of us with brains and ideas to be exchanged and never enough time. Your voice must be hoarse from cheering me on. Thank you for your reading, your truth-telling and, even more, for your friendship.

On friendship, Meg Bignell, you have walked the marathon of this book with me. And I mean walked it. A text saying 'I'm out' has me pulling on my walking shoes, ringing you and then we would talk – you striding over the downs of Bream Creek, or up the steep Hobart streets, me on the farm. A hundred kilometres from each other our conversations are always intimate and sustaining. Thank you for your belief, your humour, your fury and your loyalty. You're a treasure.

My TOGs – Amanda Bowes, Lucy Davey, Kristy Foster, Barb Sheedy, Elizabeth Turvey and Leigh Vanderkelen – you've shown me your Tasmania and gifted me the wild places and bellyfuls of laughter. I'm so grateful for our walks and your friendship.

At a time where I had lost my confidence as a writer, I turned up virtually for a Sarah Sentilles Word Cave retreat. Sarah's teaching and creation of this virtual space unlocked my writing again.

Thank you to my friend Catriona Nicholls for your steely editing eye. Your expertise as an agricultural communicator and your knowledge of the wool industry were crucial in helping me finesse my description of sheep husbandry.

My friends Sarah Bird and Jo Ackland have enriched these pages with their creativity. I watched Sarah's bird sketches slowly develop on Instagram and knew I wanted her to illustrate my bird word sketches. Jo's map brings the house and yards to life. Thank you both for your engagement and for making this little book a visual treasure.

COVID has been good to me as a regional writer. The world of Zoom has gifted me a writing group. Rafters, Bronwyn Birdsall, Meg Bignell, Jessie Cole and Carolyn Fraser – your friendship, understanding, belief and commitment to showing up in my computer screen have made this writing life a joy.

Practically, I have been supported by a Create COVID grant from the Copyright Fund and a week of retreat at Bobundara in the Monaro, donated by Trisha Dixon-Birkett and Margie Seale. Both these generous acts of financial support and space were integral to the transformation of words and ideas into a book.

My publisher Nikki Christer has been steadfast in her belief of me. Thank you for waiting, Nikki, and for your championing of my career (despite hiatuses between output). I'm so lucky to have Catherine Hill as my editor and friend. Catherine's fine eye, sensitive ear and twitchy pen searching out the purple in my prose have tightened my words and made me a better writer. Thank you to my agent, Fiona Inglis, who wept in the appropriate places and who hasn't despaired (to me, anyway) at how long this book has taken to find its feet.

Family comes in all shapes and sizes. I want to thank and acknowledge the support of Martha Bentley, Bernard Gallate and Kate Gordon. Each of you individually and all of you collectively have been as flagstones beneath me. May our lives continue to entwine and make something beautiful.

To my brothers, Cam and Duncan, who share these pages and our unusual and at times tricky childhood. Thank you for making me a middle child. Cam, your wild creativity combined with an ability to cut through all red tape make you a magical person who probably should go into politics. I'm so lucky you're my brother and I couldn't be prouder of you. Duncan, you're an extraordinary human. I've only captured a fragment of you in these pages – you are so much more. I hope, one day to write the more.

And finally, my children, Arkie and Clancy, who are grown now and have their own stories. My loves, thank you for letting me write about us; you are more magnificent than I could ever put on the page.

MAGGIE MACKELLAR is a writer and historian living on the east coast of Tasmania/lutruwita. She writes the much-loved newsletter The Sit Spot. *Graft* is her fifth book.

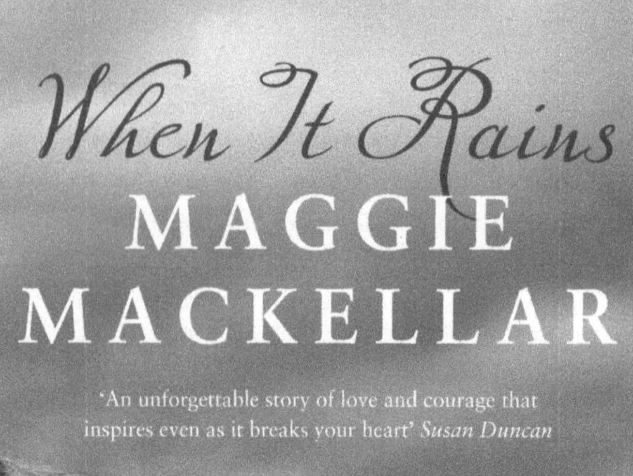
When It Rains
MAGGIE
MACKELLAR
'An unforgettable story of love and courage that inspires even as it breaks your heart' Susan Duncan

VINTAGE

When It Rains
Maggie MacKellar

The heart-wrenching but triumphant story of rebuilding a life and a family.

When Maggie MacKellar's vibrant young husband, father to a five-year-old daughter and an unborn son, dies tragically, Maggie is left widowed and due to give birth three months later to their second child.

Then her beloved mother, backbone of the family, mother to three children, grandmother to two, dies suddenly of aggressive cancer. In two short years, Maggie's life has shattered.

After a year, she gives up trying to juggle single motherhood and the demands of an academic career and returns with her children to the family farm in central western New South Wales to take stock and catch a breath.

The farm becomes a redemptive, healing place for Maggie and her children as they battle the heat and drought that only the Australian landscape can offer. She throws herself into the horses, sheep, ducks and chickens and slowly, finally, realises she has found a new shape for herself.

When It Rains is a meditation on grief and the vagaries of the human condition, and a stunning memoir about piecing back together a life, and moving forward, one step at a time.

BESTSELLING AUTHOR OF *WHEN IT RAINS*

MAGGIE MACKELLAR

how to get there

{a memoir}

VINTAGE

How to Get There
Maggie MacKellar

Maggie MacKellar's second memoir traces with her characteristic candour and perception her move to Tasmania, for love, and the struggles and joys of settling there.

In 2011 Maggie MacKellar moves from her family's farm in Central West New South Wales to the east coast of Tasmania with her children and assorted menagerie to live with a farmer.

This story takes as its epigraph a quote from Roger McDonald: 'Through every small opening in life, through the tiniest most restricted nerve ends, through rips and tears and tatters, life pours.'

In the book she explores learning to love again after living through grief, and the complexities of doing this in a community with which she is unfamiliar, with two young children. She reflects on love after grief, juggling being a mother and negotiating a burgeoning relationship, the rhythms of country life, displacement and the writing life.

This is a book for anyone who has imagined taking a risk, for anyone who has moved to a new place and struggled with feelings of homesickness and displacement. It is a story about making a life in a remarkable setting – the east coast of Tasmania, on a sheep farm in a stone house built by convicts in 1828.